PREDATOR HUNTING

PREDATOR HUNTING

A Complete Guide to Hunting Coyotes, Foxes, Bobcats, Bears, and More

BILL BYNUM

The Lyons Press
Guilford, Connecticut
An imprint of The Globe Pequot Press

The Lyons Press is an imprint of The Globe Pequot Press.

Printed in the United States of America

10 9 8 7 6 5 4 3 2 1

ISBN 1-59228-388-8

Library of Congress Cataloging-in-Publication Data is available on file.

DEDICATION

I dedicate this book to all my friends in the hunting industry: Linda, Jim, Judd, Joe, and many others. Thanks to your friendship and support a childhood dream has become reality. A special note of gratitude goes to my beloved brothers of the hunt, Craig Boddington, J. W. Fears, and David Lambert. Our adventures have been among the greatest I have known. The years have passed as quickly as the autumn leaves cast upon a flowing stream, and the countless memories are the true reflections of my career. They are times I'll cherish until the hunter's horn signals the end of this hunter's way. Then Mr. Elmer and I will light cigars, pull a cork, and discuss why the hunt never ends for those we call true friends.

CONTENTS

FOREWORD ix

Chapter 1   Why Bother Hunting Predators 1

Chapter 2   Learning from the Masters 15

Chapter 3   Philosophy of the Ultimate Predator 25

Chapter 4   Gearing Up for the Hunt 35

Chapter 5   Scouting 57

Chapter 6   Calling 75

Chapter 7   Hunting the Coyote 93

Chapter 8   Early Encounters with Coyotes 105

Chapter 9   Western Coyotes 113

Chapter 10   Thinking Differently for Eastern Predators 123

Chapter 11   Tricks of the Trade 131

Chapter 12   Weather or Not 147

Chapter 13   Hunting Anytime 155

Chapter 14   Hunting Public Land 165

Chapter 15   Hunting Foxes and Raccoons 173

Chapter 16   Hunting the Bobcat 189

Chapter 17   Hunting Large Predators 203

Chapter 18   Caring for Your Trophy 223

Index 235

FOREWORD

I was fortunate enough to have a father who was a predator hunter. Under his tutelage I learned to call fox and bobcats as a preteen youngster. He believed that in order to be a really good predator hunter you had to first be a really good predator; you had to think and move like a predator.

When I first heard about the book you hold in your hands I wondered who would be the author. Was it just another hunter/writer or was it a predator/writer? To me, that would make the difference between just another so-so hunting book and a book that was a condensed library of useful tips and insights into the world of predator hunting. I was pleased to learn the author was a predator named Bill Bynum.

I can't remember exactly when I first met Bill—that was longer ago than either of us will admit—but I can remember that our first conversation was about the eastern coyote. Bill has sharp features, and a weathered, hawk-like look that you see in paintings of early American explorers. It comes from a lifetime of living in the woods. As we discussed coyotes, Bill's eyes took in everything and his hands moved almost cat-like as he described an area of west Tennessee he wanted me to hunt with him. I sensed that my newfound friend was a predator.

Soon after that we were hunting the woods and fields where he grew up. And I saw firsthand that he really was a predator—a damn good one. He was not just another hunter; he walked the walk. Sharing camp with him was like a course in pioneering. He was a modern-day Daniel Boone, and I was glad to call him a friend.

Since those early days we have shared mountaintops and swamp bottoms, enjoying every minute of it. Bill is one of

America's top predator hunters, and he takes pleasure in passing along his vast knowledge. I have shared the stage with him at numerous hunting seminars, and there is no one more entertaining and enlightening when talking about those great animals we call predators or the skills it takes to hunt them.

So sit back and get comfortable, you are about to go to the next level of predator hunting.

J. Wayne Fears
Cross Creek Hollow, Alabama

Chapter

1

WHY BOTHER HUNTING PREDATORS

Predation is a fact of life. Man's very existence revolves around various forms of predation. Today, society often shuns those who prey on animals for food and sport. But hunting is an act as old as mankind. It's played an integral role in our evolution. While we no longer depend on our hunting skills for survival, predation does still exist.

Whether we kill animals ourselves or have someone else do it, we prey on life to sustain life. Yes, I know this is a great way to start an argument, but pork chops, pot roast, and chicken breasts aren't born within the walls of a deep freezer. Someone had to kill the cow, chicken, pig, or lamb so it could become a meal. Yet hunters are often vilified until they are needed to stop animals that have become a nuisance in the eyes of society.

History shows that the conflict between man and beast has always existed. There's been a problem since the first time some animal took something of value from humans. Perhaps it was a saber-toothed-something-or-other stealing a hunk of meat—or perhaps a family member—who knows. I've never met anyone

Predation can influence many different wildlife populations, especially among small game and birds.

praising a creature that stole something from them. These days, ranchers and farmers are usually the primary candidates for such a menace. But some other folks are also feeling the effects of predation, which we will talk more about later in this chapter.

Predation can occur in many ways, with as many victims as culprits. In most instances, we think of predation as a coyote killing a lamb or a fox stealing a chicken. These are certainly common occurrences in rural areas, but predation is not restricted to any given location or tied directly to the level of human inhabitance. So the need for controlling, or attempting to control, a predation problem can exist anywhere. A classic example of this is found within some of the largest cities in the country.

COYOTES ON CONCRETE

Los Angeles, California, is an enormous city, yet it hosts a very large coyote population. That's right; coyotes are as common on the streets of Los Angeles as traffic cops. Los Angeles County tax-payers spend thousands of dollars each year to combat coyotes. Attacks on people, even fatal ones, have been documented here.

And this isn't the only city where one might see a coyote crossing the street. In fact, any city in the coyote's range may be home to *Canis latrans*. Like humans, many coyotes seem to prefer city or suburban lifestyles to country living. Perhaps these animals feel safer dodging cars and eating garbage and pets than dodging bullets and hunting hard in the woods in order to survive. The coyote's adaptability has allowed it to flourish in areas no one would have ever thought possible. The problem, of course, is how to control a predator population inside the city limits.

In most cases, some form of Animal Damage Control program will be implemented by the city, and these problems may also fall under the jurisdiction of the local Humane Society. No

Coyotes have adapted well to suburban and urban environments, where public money must be spent to deal with them. (FWS)

matter who is given the task of dealing with such predators, funding usually comes from tax dollars. So anyone earning a living is affected by the presence of predators.

Predators, especially coyotes and foxes, are notorious for snatching pets such as cats and small dogs. This is a common occurrence in many locations across the country. Mrs. Jones lets her prize poodle out in the backyard to make a puddle. Thirty minutes later she steps out to check on the little dog, but it's nowhere to be found. In most cases, the dog will never be discovered unless someone accidentally steps in a pile of coyote scat a week later.

A number of attacks on humans in suburban areas have been documented in recent years. These attacks have usually been by cougars and bears, and some have resulted in severe injury or death for the people involved.

But according to some folks, such attacks are merely the result of the depletion of the animals' habitat, so they shouldn't be

Mountain lions often follow deer into populated areas. (Sue Weddle)

held accountable. It has launched a debate that speaks directly to how we choose to live. I don't have the perfect answer for the problem, but I do know that if I see a critter trying to harm something of mine chances are it'll be trying for its last supper.

NO MERCY

In the wild, almost any predator will feed when an opportunity presents itself. A coyote will take a rabbit as quickly as a raccoon will destroy a quail nest. It is the nature of the beast to survive; it's that simple. The problem is that predators are generally fond of the same things as man. It irritates me when I see the nest of a gamebird that contains nothing but broken eggs. And the sight of a partially eaten deer fawn makes me hunt even harder than usual for the culprits.

Livestock attacks that result in a great deal of suffering or agonizing deaths aren't uncommon. Often, these animals were the

Predators can wreak havoc on big game populations, which puts them at odds with hunters and landowners.

victims of malicious predators that didn't even stay to eat the meat. On several occasions, I've had farmers report to me that something had been chewing on the tails of their cattle. After some scouting, I usually discover that a pack of coyotes has been using the cattle for sport. This, in turn, results in me returning the favor with my rifle, restoring peace to the area for a while. Resolving problems such as these is gratifying for both the landowner and me.

Coyotes are by no means the only destructive creatures I've encountered. In fact, some of the most troublesome animals are

Domestic livestock like sheep are often the victims of predation.

actually raccoons and opossums. Both of these species can destroy an entire nest of gamebirds in a matter of minutes, whether it contains eggs or young that can't flee. Foxes are also very effective at robbing nests and capturing the young. I once watched a single red fox capture and kill seven young rabbits. The sad thing was that it only ate two of them before leaving the area. Even sadder, I was without armament and could do nothing but observe.

On another occasion, I witnessed a bobcat play cat and mouse with an injured cottontail rabbit. Nearly a quarter of an hour expired while the cat batted the little bunny around in a most hideous manner. Luckily for the bobcat, a hunting restriction prevented me from donating a bullet to a worthy cause. From experiences such as these I have learned to enjoy the victory of predator hunting even more.

ADDED DIVIDENDS

Serious predator hunters will discover that they are often people in demand. Once the folks around town discover you can deplete the local predator population you become a hot commodity. The number of calls I get summoning me to area farms would surprise you, and it sometimes leads to an interesting hunt.

One night, a woman called to inform me that a few of her family's newly born calves had been attacked by something. This was a common story, and I had little to get excited about. However, she was nice and very persistent, so I gave in.

The following morning, I was enjoying a cup of coffee with the lady and her husband after driving eighty miles or so to their ranch. They gave me a map of their four-thousand-acre haven and a master key to all the locks. Life seemed good for a moment, as it is a rarity to gain access to that type of land without a hefty price tag attached.

Soon I was driving along the gravel roads that connected the numerous pastures of the ranch. I was amazed at the number of scat piles I saw, and at all the wild turkeys, deer, and other game present. But I was here to live up to my obligation by collecting coyotes.

The collecting started fairly quickly when I noticed a coyote slowly walking across one of the pastures. After taking this freebee I made the first call of the day. In minutes I had raised the score to three.

A sense of pride flowed through me when I saw the owner's pickup coming down the road. Within seconds of seeing the departed coyotes in the bed of my truck, the gentleman was having a celebration. Never had I dreamed that this predator hunt would open the doors to some of the best hunting lands I'd ever see, but that's exactly what happened. Just another dividend that pursuing predators can provide for the enterprising hunter.

Removing harmful animals is a great way to cement long-term hunter/landowner relations.

POLITICS AND PREDATION

Today, there is a great debate rising in several of the western states revolving around the reintroduction of the gray wolf into Wyoming, Montana, and Idaho. This conflict is an excellent example of how politics can affect wildlife conservation and management.

During the 1800s, wolves were numerous in the West. In fact, these animals often wreaked havoc on livestock and wildlife alike. In 1884 Montana placed a bounty on wolves, and in 1915 the federal government began a wolf-eradication program. By 1925, western wolf populations were negligible.

But in 1944 Aldo Leopold began pushing for wolf-restoration programs across the West. And in 1974 the wolf was listed as an endangered species under the federal Endangered Species Act of 1973.

The gray wolf was a favorite target in the early days of the West. By the early 1900s, they were virtually eliminated in the lower 48 states. (FWS)

The first documented livestock kill by a wolf in fifty years occurred in 1980. The U.S. government killed the wolf. Then, in 1986, the "Magic Pack" was discovered in Glacier National Park, and so named because it was the first pack to be documented in the West in over half a century.

In 1991, the U.S Fish and Wildlife Service, under Congressional direction, drafted the Environmental Impact Statement on Wolf Recovery in Yellowstone National Park and Idaho. By 1994, the draft was finalized: wolves were to be reintroduced in Yellowstone and Idaho for three to five years as "experimental, nonessential" populations. Wolf recovery included thirty breeding pairs being released in Montana, Idaho, and Wyoming for three successive years.

After several transplants of Canadian wolves, Idaho and Yellowstone populations numbered 163. In 1998, the federal government proposed changing the wolf's status from endangered

This is a sight not seen in the American West for many years, but it might soon be commonplace once again. (Sue Weddle)

to threatened. And in 2001 Montana passed legislation reclassifying the gray wolf as "a species in need of management," which would allow people to defend themselves and their property against wolf attacks. In 2003 the U.S. Fish and Wildlife Service proposed reclassifying gray wolves in the Rocky Mountain area, not including experimental, nonessential populations, from endangered to threatened, which would allow for more flexible management.

Now that we've reviewed some of the high points in the restoration of the gray wolf into the West, let's ask ourselves a question. Why? Why would the U.S government want to return this large predator to these areas? I can see the point of not having the wolf become extinct, but why place this four-legged killing machine among some of the finest elk herds left in the country? Why place the wolf on lands that have been managed to increase moose populations? Why use tax dollars and money

In recent years, the federal government has released Canadian wolves in Yellowstone National Park and Idaho. (FWS)

generated by sportsmen to increase game populations and then bring in wolves?

Just like some of the laws governing hunting, this makes no sense to me. Many of these laws were created by people who need to spend more time in the field to see how predation is really affecting specific areas. And some of these laws bind the hands of hunters who aren't likely to have a significant effect on predator populations, anyway. This is why I urge every hunter to know exactly where a politician stands before giving him or her a vote.

LOVE OF THE GAME

Predator hunting has a lot of benefits, not the least of which is the fact that it allows me to hunt more often. Predator hunting also gives me a feeling of great satisfaction when I'm successful and a desire to do better when I'm not.

Camaraderie is one of the many rewards of predator hunting.

Like everything found in nature, each species of predator is unique in its own way. For example, some predators have a better olfactory capability, while others possess a higher level of intelligence. But the one characteristic they all share is the natural instinct to hunt. These animals utilize their hunting skills almost every waking moment of their lives.

Therefore, when we pursue these animals we are competing against some of the finest hunters nature has ever developed. This is another reason I love the sport of predator hunting; the pleasure of knowing I have beaten one of the best at its own game.

Chapter

2

LEARNING FROM
THE MASTERS

Growing up in rural western Tennessee had many advantages. My playground extended for as far as the eye could see. My sandbox was a dry creekbed that winded for miles under towering trees. The many large vines I used to cross the creeks (or fall into them) during the summer months served as my swing set. My monkey bars consisted of tree limbs that guided me to homemade deer stands. Any hollow log was an adventurous tunnel or shelter from sudden rain. When unencumbered by the burdens of chores and school, I was at home in the outdoors.

My thirst for hunting began at a very early age, when my late uncle, Gene Hicks, began taking me into the woods. Squirrels were our primary target, and my youthful eyes aided him in achieving our goal. After a few years my grandfather began allowing me to carry a .22 rifle. I began hunting solo at the age of six.

Safety was my grandfather's highest priority, and it quickly became a religion of sorts. Marksmanship also ranked high on his list. My allotment of three .22 Shorts was parceled out daily. And for every squirrel collected, I received a bonus of three additional cartridges. If the squirrel received a headshot an additional two cartridges fell into the kitty.

Ammunition was stored in a pull-string cloth tobacco pouch, and my beloved single-shot rifle was cleaned with pride at the end of each day. Granddad would sharpen my Barlow pocketknife on a weekly basis. He was a firm believer in "you shoot it, you skin it." Before I knew it, I was becoming a fairly decent hunter under my granddad's guidance.

Sickness had taken away the use of his legs long before I was born, but his stern lessons directed me on every hunt. Additional instruction also came through reading about the exploits of my idols. I literally wore the ink off the pages of *Outdoor Life, Field and Stream,* and other hunting magazines. My young mind immortalized the names of Elmer Keith, John Wootters, and Warren Page. It was also in these pages that I discovered the names of Murray and Winston Burnham, men who would launch my craving to hunt predators.

BECOMING A HERO

Chickens were highly valued on the farm, and my grandmother nearly worshiped her Rhode Island Reds. She despised any animal that threatened a chicken or its eggs. This included snakes, hawks, possums, dogs, and most of all, foxes.

Most people hated foxes, both red and gray. Quail and rabbit hunters often railed against the damage foxes did to the local populations. The only exceptions to this rule were the men who enjoyed listening to their dogs chasing a fox all night. These folks were labeled "foxhunters" by the locals and generally derided behind their backs if not to their faces. The majority of the local population felt every fox should be shot on sight, hopefully before it left its mother's breast. So when I had my first encounter with a very poor looking red, I became a hero.

The day of my first predator kill is still fresh in my memory. Granddad had allowed me to go squirrel hunting before doing the chores. The first light of dawn found me hunched beneath a hickory tree. The unfortunate fox traveled within ten yards or so of my spot, stopped to look at the funny object, then caught a .22 between its eyes.

Immediately after the villain dropped, I reloaded and put another round into its ear from point-blank range. Then I hastily dragged the corpse home to receive the praise I knew I'd get from my grandparents, who were eating breakfast.

Soon the celebration was over and as I joined them at the table my grandfather gave me a dollar bill as a reward. This would buy me two boxes of Shorts or a box of high-powered Long Rifle cartridges, with change left over. I opted for the latter, as I sensed the need for power in the upcoming days.

In my youth, bringing home a red fox was always cause for celebration.

The upgrade in ammunition gave me my first lesson in ballistics. The new cartridges changed my rifle's point of impact. After I missed a couple of squirrels my granddad taught me a few things about trajectory.

GETTING STARTED

A couple of years had passed since the day of my first fox. During this time my granddad lost his battle against cancer, and I was already fulfilling the obligations of early manhood. Hunting had now become an obsession, and the normal things other kids did only bored me. The price of a movie could buy ammo, and girls just seemed like trouble in my book. The result of all this was that most of my friends were neighboring farmers many times my age. One old gentleman taught me the pleasure of listening to hounds pursuing a raccoon, while regaling me with tales of World War II. I learned a lot of valuable information from these men, especially when it came to hunting, fishing, trapping, and dogs. The art of tracking I had pretty much learned on my own, and it was something that truly fascinated me.

This same fascination also applied to game calling. My introduction to calling began with a P.S. Olt crow caller my uncle had given me. It took a while for me to learn the bird's language, but I did, which quickly proved to be a nightmare for the local crow population.

My next lesson came when a neighbor invited me to join him on a foxhunting expedition. This basically meant I would hold the six-cell flashlight while he called and did the shooting from the bed of his pickup. I found this exciting but resented the fact that I was not receiving any trigger time. So after spotting a magazine ad, I became the proud owner of a Burnham Brothers predator caller.

The caller quickly became a prized possession, and through trial and error I managed to collect a few fox pelts. However, it was not until I made friends with a gentleman called Ol' Tom that I learned how it was really done.

FUELING THE FIRE

Tom was a well-known sportsman in the area and a great lover of quail hunting. So any animal that might harm a quail was dead meat in Tom's eyes. This was especially true for the ever-hated fox.

My first outing with Ol' Tom proved to be an eye opener. The old man picked me up one chilly afternoon just minutes after I stepped off the school bus. In no time, I transferred from duds to gear and we were soon traveling along a gravel road. During the ride the old man silently smoked his pipe. I became a little nervous, wondering why I had even been invited.

Soon we came to a slow stop near a freshly harvested cornfield. Here, Tom stepped from the truck and retrieved his Model 12 Winchester shotgun from the gun rack. I thought this would be an appropriate time to compliment his gun and show my appreciation for the invitation. Wrong! Before I could finish my opening sentence the old man's sneering voice silenced me. He narrowed his eyes while growling at me, and I quickly got the idea that he wasn't the least bit happy. To add insult to injury, he told me, still in his whispering growl, to leave my gun in the truck.

Feeling like an abused stepchild, I followed the old man along the edge of the field. Twice he stopped, gathered a handful of powdery dirt, and inspected the breeze. When he found an angle where the dust settled in his face, we took up a position inside the fencerow bordering the field.

Ol' Tom handed me a pair of brown jersey gloves with the fingertips removed and a piece of green cloth to cover my face. He quickly donned a similar outfit. These items, in conjunction with the old man's WWII camouflage-patterned jacket, created his disguise.

Ol' Tom

He slowly stuffed three rounds of No. 2 buckshot into the shotgun and checked the safety. Then he retrieved the callers from inside his jacket. This immediately gained my attention, as I noted three different types. Hanging from the homemade lanyard I noted the P.S. Olt predator caller (long range), a Burnham Brothers (medium range), and a caller that looked like some kind of magnum Popsicle stick. The latter, I eventually discovered, was a call he had made himself from two tongue depressors and some rubber bands. He used this as a close-range coaxer.

Within minutes of his blowing the medium-range caller, a single gray fox had met its fate. Ol' Tom wasted no time in giving the fox a barrelful of buckshot, but his only reaction to the shot was to reload the gun and start another calling sequence.

I sat patiently beside the old man, listening while he played the bunny blues with the caller. I thought this was pretty funny, as I knew every animal in the area must have heard the eruption of the shotgun. Maybe the old man was losing it. But after about fifteen minutes or so he suddenly snapped the gun in place and sent another dose of buckshot on its way. Where this second gray fox came from I still haven't figured out, but it did come—and it died just as quickly as the first.

Ol' Tom then shucked the shells from the gun and stood up. He lit his beloved pipe while instructing me to gather the catch. This would become our standard routine for several weeks to come: Tom having all the fun while I watched and did the dirty work. However, the old man always divided the catch equally, and fur meant money in those days.

Tom and I remained friends for several years before his sudden passing while sitting in a duck blind. I often think of him and his willingness to share his wealth of knowledge with me. He enjoyed it, despite his gruff exterior. His uncanny knack for predicting what an animal would do still baffles me. I continue to benefit from his lessons every time I go afield. Tom was one of the greatest "sign readers" and hunters I have ever known.

THE IMMORTALS

In retrospect, I wish I had studied my schoolbooks a little harder than my beloved hunting magazines. But that's life, and it was my own fault. Still, I have no regrets about the heroes I chose to emulate. Professional athletes didn't inspire me at all, but the feats of professional hunters had my full attention. This was especially true of the Burnham Brothers, Jim Dougherty, Johnny Stewart, and anyone else who wrote about predator hunting. These men conquered countless coyotes, bobcats, and cougars.

The only problem was that few, if any, of these predators called western Tennessee home. So I had to make do, and foxes remained my primary targets. Sure, someone claimed to see a bobcat now and then, but foxes were the mainstay.

The lessons I learned from the magazines, or thought I had learned, were always put to use, which is why I saved money for several months to acquire an electronic game-calling machine. My youthful ego would soon take some powerful licks as a result.

The Bounty Hunter calling machine's fragile design could be a real pain, especially in cold weather. The unit also ate D-cell batteries like a rich kid ate candy. Add in the fact that the short-playing

Tactics that bring down western coyotes don't always work on eastern predators.

45-rpm records usually stopped just about the time a fox showed up, and you can see why I chalked this up as an expensive failure.

The magazine articles also taught me that what works in one part of the country doesn't necessarily work everywhere. The tricks I garnered from the grand masters weren't netting the same kind of results I'd seen with Ol' Tom's methods. The reason for this, I later realized, was that I had been trying to use western methods for hunting eastern critters. The instructions I was following were primarily for calling coyotes and bobcats, not foxes. Looking back, I guess maybe I was ahead of my time. Or maybe I was just beginning to view predator hunting as more of a science than a sport.

Chapter

3

PHILOSOPHY OF THE ULTIMATE PREDATOR

There was a time when the old saying "man is the ultimate predator" probably held a lot of merit. Killing a beast many times your size and strength with nothing but a sharp rock had to be gratifying—if you survived. Think about how you would feel knowing that the critter you were throwing stones at wanted to kill you, too. One little slip and *you* end up as dinner instead.

Today, few types of hunting really place humans in any kind of real jeopardy, although it's still a dangerous activity. You can die while hunting without a lion grabbing you by the throat. In fact, people die every year while pursuing game that's trying desperately to avoid them. Heart attacks, gun accidents, and just plain negligence claim plenty of lives.

Negligence is the greatest single factor leading to disaster, in my opinion. The things we neglect to do almost always come back to haunt us. This is especially true with modern man, due to our relatively easy lifestyle.

In the old days, free time in the evening was generally spent preparing for the next day's challenges. These days, our evenings

Solid hunting skills and attention to detail lead to success like this.

are filled with the distractions of television, cell phones, and a dizzying array of other electronic gadgets. I think people now tend to rely more on convenience and luck than brains and skill. Some hunters I know never even give preparation a thought.

HUNTING PARTNERS

Having a good hunting partner can be a real pleasure. "Good" means doing a fair share of the work and always thinking for success. A good hunting partner is one you can count on when the chips are down. They never complain if a calling stand turns sour or if the last cup of coffee is lukewarm. The companionship of a true partner increases the enjoyment of the hunt. I know this because I've had some really fine partners over the years.

Clay Stuckey is a guy I love to hunt with. When we first met, Clay was somewhat of a novice about hunting the eastern coyote.

But he wanted to learn everything he could about the animal. Most of all, Clay knew the importance of always forming some kind of hunting strategy. In fact, Clay was one of the few hunters I've ever partnered with that I trusted completely. He was also one of the few that figured out one of my philosophies without having to be shown.

Clay and I were hunting a piece of public land for the second time in two weeks when he noticed I was returning to the same areas as the previous hunt. Having read some articles that claimed this wasn't a good idea, he questioned my method.

Our first outing had consisted of an entire morning with never a shot fired. We had seen plenty of fresh signs, but had not laid an eye on anything. And the weather had been what I consider perfect: cold and clear, with barely any wind. Our lack of success troubled me for the better part of a week. Why weren't the animals responding to the caller? Should we have been hunting somewhere else?

There hadn't been any sign of other hunter-related activity in the area, so I doubted that the animals had become wise to calling. In the end, I trusted my instincts and did what the sign I found told me to do—come back again.

As we repeated the course, the second calling site found me staring into the eyes of a lone coyote. Unfortunately for the coyote, I was looking through my riflescope, and it quickly became the first kill of the day. At the next stand, Clay was charged by a pack of three coyotes, which he quickly reduced to one. Stand after stand, we repeated our previous course, whacking critters like clockwork.

I knew I hadn't imagined all those signs of game. Why the first outing transpired as it did, I'll never know. But I stuck to my philosophy; the signs showed the animals were there and that's all that mattered.

Clay Stuckey shows proof of a sound hunting philosophy.

HUNTING RIGS

Sadly, few predator hunters, especially those in the eastern portion of the country, think about their hunting vehicles. If the vehicle runs, they figure it's sufficient for hunting. These hunters never give a thought to problems until after they occur. Not me, brother. My pickup is my palace when I leave home.

Taking a little time to check the air pressure in your tires, and the spare tire, can save you a lot of trouble. The same goes for the oil and fluids for the transmission, brakes, and power steering. A quick inspection of the water in your battery may save a long walk when the motor won't start. The same inspection should also include the battery terminals. Cleaning corroded terminals in a downpour is not my idea of fun. I also check the tire jack regularly and lubricate it as needed.

Inside the glove box of my truck, along with the air pressure gauge, are two boxes of assorted fuses, a flashlight, spare batteries, two disposable cigarette lighters, and a first-aid kit. Behind the seat is a compact blanket, an extra set of clothes, including socks, and some canned food with a can opener in a sealed bag. Food items consist of ready-to-eat stuff and a couple of cans of soup. People with the habit will also note that this is a good place to store an extra pack of smokes.

In the toolbox or trunk, I keep an assortment of wrenches, screwdrivers, and a pair of adjustable pliers. I also carry spare parts, jumper cables, two cans of Fix-a-Flat, and a can of quality spray lubricant. A box of heavy-duty trash bags sits atop a short-handled shovel and hatchet.

Spare ammunition, callers, extra facemasks, camouflage gloves, a roll of paper towels, and a gallon of water are also included. The rubber boots I bring have come in handy on occasions, too. Duct taping a spare key somewhere on the vehicle's frame can also save a lot of frustration.

The key is to plan for the unexpected, which eliminates the worries of *what if* and allows you to think about more important things, such as killing critters.

CONDITIONING

Physical conditioning is something I feel most hunters neglect. In fact, most of us don't even think about it until we begin to feel the effects of a long day of hunting. This is especially true during periods of extreme cold, when the hunting usually gets really good. Hunters with silver in their hair or known health problems should never discount the possibility of stroke or heart attack.

Advancing age has made me think a bit more about my physical well-being. Today, I view things differently than I once did. Those long, steep hills I used to run right up now seem a lot longer and steeper. I've learned to take it easy and enjoy the day, and I'm less burdened by sore muscles as a result. Staying active year-round helps, as well.

Like a lot of you, I make most of my living sitting behind a desk, in front of a computer with a phone stuck in my ear. The only real exercise this provides is in my jaw and finger muscles. However, I have learned that with the aid of a portable telephone I can exercise while I work—squatting, bending, and stretching. When hunting season rolls around, the aches and pains of all-day exertions are minimal. Every little bit helps.

Technology, such as cell phones and two-way radios, has also made life easier and safer for the hunter. So why do so many hunters neglect to bring these possibly life-saving devices when they go afield?

Protecting your body also includes leaving a map or itinerary with someone in case of emergency. I often wonder how many

Those long treks into prime hunting country are much easier when you're in shape.

lives could have been saved over the years if the victims had just jotted down their probable route and left it with a friend or loved one. Think about it the next time you plan a hunt.

GAINING THE MENTAL EDGE

Superstitions have never really influenced my thinking. In fact, Friday the thirteenths are generally good days for me, if I even notice them. Black cats only get my attention when they are in the wild, where the only bad luck is usually theirs. So why do I feel so strongly about the mental aspect of hunting? Because I believe our attitudes influence our behavior.

Hunting is as much a mental game as it is a physical one. If our minds aren't completely focused on what we're doing the margin of error increases. We should be fully consumed by the existing environment and nothing else. Full concentration is a critical element in detecting the slightest movement, which can determine success or failure.

Mental preparation should also consist of getting in tune with ourselves. Bringing your everyday attitude into the woods is a recipe for disaster. The fast pace we must maintain to live in the modern world doesn't translate well to the natural world. A good example of this is simply how some people walk. The most common human stride is hurried and heavy-footed. But few, if any, animals travel through the woods in this manner unless frightened. So why send alarm bells ringing through the forest before you even begin your hunt?

Staying relaxed and focused allows you to notice things you might otherwise miss. Things like the distant squawking of a blue jay or squirrel; sounds you might not pay attention to if you are thinking about something other than hunting. These sounds often alert a hunter to the fact that a predator is responding to the

Keeping your head in the game at all times will provide you with more opportunities afield.

sounds of the caller, providing precious time to prepare for the moment of truth even before the animal is in sight.

"Practice makes perfect" is one of my favorite sayings. This is why I develop methods for practicing everything I can. Some of my practice techniques could be defined as daydreaming, but they're much more than that. I simply forget about anything but hunting by directing my mind away from everything else. These mental practice sessions help me train myself to switch on and off the hassles of daily life when I go hunting. Some people might think this is impossible, or even foolish, but don't knock it until you've really tried it for a few weeks. In fact, if you are thinking about hunting as much as I am, you might already be doing it unconsciously.

Firearm safety should always be the top priority of every hunter, and this is another reason why our minds must be clear of any distractions. I have had clients walk beside me with unsafe guns on any number of occasions. Nine times out of ten, the handler was unaware of his actions because he was thinking of something else. I find this very irritating. Anyone carrying a deadly weapon must take responsibility for its use. Your head has to be in the game.

Chapter

4

GEARING UP FOR THE HUNT

The type of equipment we use for hunting predators plays a major role in our success. In most instances, the same equipment used for other types of hunting, such as clothing and firearms, will be adequate for hunting predators. But the devices we use for calling predators don't really apply to hunting other species. (One of the few exceptions is a turkey call, which can work on predators at times.)

In recent years, numerous advancements have been made in the predator-hunting market. This is particularly true of the firearms, ammunition, and calling devices now available. Equipment designed solely for those who pursue the sport of predator hunting has serious implications. These developments have resulted from the ever-increasing number of people pursuing predators, hence the market for such specific products. In short, the predator hunter is no longer viewed as the redheaded stepchild of the hunting industry.

PREDATOR RIFLES

The right rifle can add to the pleasure we take in a day afield, as well as the harvest. The weight and balance of a rifle are

Modern gear makes hunting more comfortable, but it still takes knowledge and experience to bring home a cagey coyote.

important factors that should never be overlooked. There are other important aspects as well, but these two are critical in my opinion. They directly affect the shooter's maneuverability with the rifle and his ability to carry the gun comfortably in a variety of conditions for short or long periods.

Rifles that are chambered for popular predator cartridges are still generally labeled as varmint rifles. Webster's describes a varmint as a "dangerous or troublesome animal," and all predators basically fit this definition. The gun industry usually categorizes a varmint as any critter capable of being shot from a sitting position with little physical effort. So varmint rifles are often designed for extensive long-range shooting from a rested position. A heavy barrel is used to reduce heating during repetitive shooting. The barrel is seated in a heavy stock, and often fitted with a heavy, high-magnification riflescope. These are great instruments for shooting at stationary targets over long distances.

Choosing a good rifle will play a critical role in the results of the hunt.

But predator hunters may find themselves packing a rifle several miles over the course of a hunt. And unlike the varmint hunter, a predator hunter may have only a split second to snap the gun into place to make a shot. A predator hunter may also need to hit a running target. Therefore, varmint-hunting rifles aren't usually a great choice for the predator hunter.

Practical predator hunting rifles were first produced by custom gun builders like Mark Bansner, H. S. Precision, E. R. Shaw, Johnny Mosley, and others. Early predator hunters had to pony up for a custom-built rifle or go on steroids in order to carry the heavier rifles then available. These custom rifles always proved to be superb in accuracy and overall performance, but like a tailored coat, they were usually created to fit an individual shooter.

Today, the gun industry has finally recognized predator hunters, and rifles are now specifically designed to meet their needs. These rifles are lighter, shorter, more accurate, and easier to handle than ever before. They also sport shorter barrels, specialized stocks, and other features. Improved rifles allow predator hunters to enjoy their sport just like the rest of the hunting world. With the wide range of rifles on the market these days, predator hunters can focus on other aspects, like the gun's action type, cartridge selection, brand name, and price.

THE RIGHT ACTION

I really don't want to spend much time on the subject of rifle actions for predators. Nine out of ten rifles found in the hands of a predator hunter will be bolt-actions. Rifles with this action are usually the most accurate, the least trouble to maintain, and the most affordable. However, some hunters prefer a semi-auto or lever gun. I even know some very serious hunters who use nothing but a single shot. The key is to find an action you are comfort-

Bolt-action rifles are far and away the most common.

able with and learn to use it well. This means practice, practice, and more practice.

Hunters should practice with the rifle whenever possible, and become familiar with all of its characteristics. In many ways, a rifle is an extension of the hunter's hands and eyes, so it should match the hunter's physical features like an article of clothing. If the rifle isn't comfortable or doesn't fit the hunter (e.g., stock length, trigger pull, etc.), it should be altered to do so. A visit to a reputable gunsmith will usually put you on the right track.

PREDATOR CARTRIDGES

The most popular cartridges used for predator hunting contain a .22-caliber (.224-inch diameter) bullet, better known as the .22-caliber centerfire. The .224-diameter bullet is found in several different cartridges, with a vast array of loadings for each. So hunters should be able to find loads that fit their specific hunting needs. Those who enjoy reloading their own ammunition can increase this selection even further.

Predator cartridges are not restricted to the .224 diameter. In fact, many hunters rely on big game cartridges such as the .243, .25/06, and .270 Winchester. These cartridges are good selections for long-range shooting or for coping with wind drift.

The basic difference in these cartridges lies in the amount of velocity they produce. Velocity is the speed of a projectile (bullet) while in flight, measured in feet per second at a specific point during the projectile's flight. These measurements usually begin at the gun's muzzle and continue downrange.

The projectile's flight path is called its trajectory. Hunters should know the

It's always a good idea to test different loads before taking to the woods.

trajectory of the designated cartridge and specific load they are using. Most hunters prefer flat-shooting cartridges that offer the least amount of bullet drop over a distance that generally matches field conditions.

The velocity a cartridge generates is determined by the type and amount of propellant used to load the cartridge. Various propellants produce various degrees of accuracy in a specific cartridge, which is one of the reasons it's so important to test different kinds of ammunition before hunting season.

The weight and design of the bullet also influence the end result of a shot, because they determine the amount of kinetic energy that will be transferred on impact.

The combination of these factors represents a load's terminal ballistics. Finding the right combination of powder and lead begins with research. Understanding what various loads do in a specific cartridge will save you a lot of trouble later on.

And remember to factor in animal size, average shooting range, and general accuracy. The size of the animal can make a big difference in what cartridge to select, as small bodies don't usually match up well with high levels of kinetic energy.

The best cartridge choice is the one you shoot with confidence and accuracy.

BALANCING THE BALLISTICS

Let's review some of the most popular predator-hunting cartridges. The family of .22-caliber centerfire cartridges contains numerous examples: the .22 Hornet, .218 Bee, .221 Fireball, .222 Remington, .222 Remington Magnum, .223 Remington, .22/250 Remington, .220 Swift, and others. Every cartridge is a good cartridge in one way or another.

The eternal question is, which one is the best? Well, there is no perfect answer. Cartridges that work well on one animal may not be satisfactory for another. For example, the .222 Remington cartridge has been popular for hunters chasing foxes and bobcats. However, many serious hunters find the triple duce inadequate for big furry coyotes. This is especially true if the coyote is beyond one hundred yards. Even with a heavy bullet, the little cartridge simply lacks the power to do the job most hunters expect. On the other

The .223 and .22/250 Remington cartridges are among the most popular for predator hunting.

hand, the larger, more powerful .22/250 Remington easily drops the larger coyote, but often transforms a little fox into a gory mess.

Okay, so if one is too light and the other too much, why not go with something in between, like the .223 Remington? This has always been a popular cartridge among predator hunters, and rightfully so. But could the .223 be just a little too heavy for the fox and a little light for the coyote? The questions never end. I myself used to lose sleep pondering cartridge choice.

Today, I don't spend much time thinking about it, as experience has prevailed in many ways. My cartridge of choice is simply the one that gives me the best accuracy for the given hunting conditions. For most coyotes and bobcats, this will be the .22/250 Remington. The .223 Remington is next in line. The basic difference between the two is case capacity. The case of the .22/250 is larger, thus capable of holding more propellant, which in turn

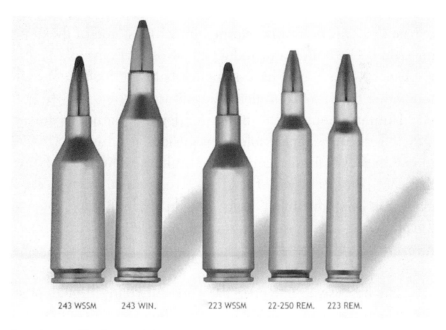

243 WSSM   243 WIN.   223 WSSM   22-250 REM.   223 REM.

Some hunters like the new "Short Magnum" cartridges.

generates higher velocities. I would rather have the power available than wish for it. Besides, the combination of velocity, bullet placement, and bullet performance will determine the outcome.

Some hunters might be wondering how the new super-short cartridges compare to the old standbys. Having used them, I can't find any negative aspects except maybe for their availability. Both the .223 and .243 Winchester Super-Short Magnum cartridges perform extremely well. But I also wouldn't say these cartridges are the best things to ever come along.

THE ALL-IMPORTANT BULLET

The projectile plays an important role in the final results of a shot. If the bullet performs properly, and hits the right spot, the critter drops in its tracks and the hunter will have to search to find the bullet hole.

Bullets today are far better than those of previous generations. One that is very popular these days features a polycarbonate tip. This tip resists deformation while stored in the gun's magazine. The bullets are produced by Nosler (Ballistic Tip) and Hornady (V-Max), and have a higher ballistic coefficient than most other bullets of equivalent size and weight.

Hunters should note, however, that polycarbonate-tipped bullets generally create violent expansion. This is due to the ultra-thin jacket formed around the bullet's mouth. I've found that shot placement with these bullets is critical. This is especially true when the bullet's velocity is on the high side. A shot to the chest of a coyote usually results in a single bullet-sized puncture, but one hitting areas with less resistance increases pelt damage dramatically.

The best way to find out what works for you is through practice, which is why I like to test my ammo on critters before the fur becomes prime. Testing and recording the results will give the

Experience is the key to selecting the right bullet for a specific type of shooting.

hunter a better idea of what the performance will be in a given gun in specific conditions.

THE DON'T-LEAVE-HOME-WITHOUT-IT CARTRIDGE

In my opinion, the most overlooked predator cartridge is the .22 Long Rifle rimfire. While this cartridge isn't usually recommended for most common predators, it is possibly the most popular backup cartridge. And the .22 rimfire has always been a top choice of hunters and trappers for dispatching downed game.

Pistols are generally the preferred type of firearm for this chambering. A .22-caliber rimfire handgun is easy to carry in a hip or shoulder holster and has many other applications in the field, not the least of which is dealing with poisonous snakes. In fact, a .22-caliber pistol has protected me and helped feed me all in the same afternoon. I don't go afield without one.

THE OTHER RIMFIRES

Predator hunters may also find a need for two other rimfire cartridges: the .22 Winchester Rimfire Magnum and the .17 Remington rimfire. With proper bullet placement, both are potent little cartridges that will turn the lights out on almost any critter.

The .22 WRM has always been a popular cartridge among varmint hunters, particularly fox and raccoon hunters. It's capable of muzzle velocities of 2,000 feet per second with a 33-grain bullet. Recent advancements in this cartridge include the use of polycarbonate bullets. In a nutshell, this is a splendid cartridge for smaller predators.

The new kid on the block is the .17 Hornady Magnum Rimfire. This cartridge generates a reported muzzle velocity of 2,550 fps with a 17-grain bullet. This is over 500 fps more than most .22 WRM loads, which sounds pretty impressive. However, let's not forget the difference in bullet weights and how bullet weight affects the energy, or killing power, downrange. In this category, the .17 is a loser. It might be an adequate cartridge for punching paper, but it's not my choice for any predator larger than a rat.

OPTICS

Predator rifles are usually fitted with scopes that provide some level of magnification. The scope primarily aids the hunter in shot placement, and in many ways is as important as the rifle itself.

There are two basic types of scopes: fixed power and variable power. The fixed-power scope is just what it sounds like, a scope set permanently at a specific magnification. Variable-power scopes allow the hunter to adjust the magnification within designated settings. This can sometimes be helpful when you must deal with a variety of field conditions.

In most predator situations, especially in areas where shots average 150 yards or less, the fixed power is a good choice. The

Scopes make pinpoint shot placement possible.

shooter can become accustomed to the designated magnification, which gives him an advantage when adjusting for the bullet's trajectory at a specific range. But lower magnifications enable the shooter to detect small obstructions that could deflect the bullet. So which type do I use? Most of the scopes I own are variable power, but I tend to set them on a specific magnification and leave them alone. I can get comfortable shooting at a consistent magnification, but if conditions suddenly change, I can adjust. Variable scopes simply offer more for the money. I recommend something in the 4X to 8X range.

It pays to research the various brands before settling on a riflescope. The construction of the scope should be a major consideration. Visit a reputable dealer, and compare models. Just like the people who use them, each optic brand is different. This is particularly true of the scope's reticle. Some reticles provide different features than others, and it's important to make sure you're comfortable with what's on your scope. Hunters who take the time to weigh all the available options generally come away with the best scope they can afford.

Binoculars are also important to the predator hunter. In fact, I view my compact binoculars as an essential part of my equipment. Compact binoculars enable me to check for "boogers" safely and increase my annual harvest.

Boogers are things we think we see but aren't quite sure about—a pair of eyes staring from behind a bush or the tip of a pointy ear barely visible in some tall grass. Little things that suddenly disappear while we're questioning our eyesight.

I don't like toting larger binoculars or spotting scopes around in the field, as I've never found them necessary. It pays to buy high-quality binoculars, however, even though the price can be steep. If you find a light, durable, comfortable pair you'll use them for many years to come.

A set of compact binoculars can help you spot game at a distance, allowing ample time to prepare for the shot.

SHOOTING AIDS

A hunter will usually get only one shot at any type of predator, so he must make the most of every opportunity. The use of a shooting aid can often be the deciding factor in whether we skin fur or not.

The most common supports are shooting sticks and bipods. A shooting stick can consist of anything from a single forked tree limb to one of the lightweight commercial devices. Basically, anything that allows the gun to be steadied can serve as a shooting stick.

Bipods are attached to the rifle's forearm and generally feature retractable limbs. They are excellent for shooting from a prone position. Various brands and models of both types of support are available, and I highly recommend those from Harris.

Your accuracy will improve if you shoot from a stable position. This hunter is using bipods to shoot from prone.

When hunting in open terrain, a rangefinder is another shooting aid worth owning. These devices allow the hunter to quickly establish the exact distance to an animal or object. Rangefinders are available from several manufacturers and in a range of prices. The most impressive units I've used are made by Bushnell and Swarovski. The key with rangefinders is to use them *before* the animal arrives, not after. Note the distance to various objects within the hunting perimeter and use these as reference points when the animal appears.

SHOTGUNS

The type of gun a hunter uses should be dictated by the terrain, which is why I often prefer a smoothbore to a rifle. In certain situations, multiple projectiles are more effective than a single one. A good example of this is when a target is moving rapidly through heavy brush. A shotgun is also a good choice when there's a possibility of close-range shooting at multiple targets. The rapid-fire capability of an autoloader or pump shotgun makes these guns a better choice than a slower-shooting bolt-action rifle at times.

Shotguns used for predators should be chambered for 3- or 3½-inch magnum shells. Predators are tough animals to kill and magnum-velocity loads usually get the job done. The best size shot will vary depending on the size of the intended target. When dealing with large predators like coyotes and bobcats, buckshot is recommended where legal (some states regulate shot size). Otherwise, use the largest shot size possible.

The choke of the shotgun should produce a dense pattern with the selected shot size at twenty-five yards. Only testing will confirm the right combination for your shotgun, but in most instances a full or modified choke works nicely. Proceed with caution when attempting to shoot large pellet sizes through special choke systems designed for turkey and waterfowl hunting. It

In close-range shooting situations, shotguns are often a good choice.

helps to know how dense your shot pattern will be out to around fifty yards, but again, only practice will reveal this.

HANDGUNS

Hunters who enjoy using handguns will find any predator a worthy opponent. Specialized handguns like the Thompson/Center Encore or Contender are chambered in various popular predator cartridges. These guns come in a variety of barrel lengths and can be easily scoped.

The lightweight Encore or Contender also makes an excellent secondary, or backup, gun for the shotgunner and bowhunter. These shooters must take close-range shots, and it pays to have another weapon in reserve. Numerous coyotes have stopped just beyond the range of my pellets or bow only to die at the crack of my Encore chambered in .22/250.

Handguns are very effective on predators when conditions are right.

HUNTING CLOTHES

Prevailing weather conditions and common sense should dictate clothing choices. And comfort should be a key factor. Generally, the clothing used for other types of hunting works well for predators, with the exception of bright colors like hunter orange.

Camouflage is the standard style for predator hunters. I wear full camouflage clothing, a facemask, and gloves, and even cover my gun. The specific camouflage pattern isn't very important, though, except in snow. Some patterns do blend better with certain types of terrain than others, but I don't worry about it too much. I actually believe the camouflage affects the hunter more than the hunted. In fact, I have hunted with some people who put more emphasis on their camouflage than their calling. They fault the camouflage style for alerting an approaching animal when in fact their own movement or hunting technique was the problem.

The author has become a fan of the Bushrag Ghillie Suit.

Camouflage patterns do build hunter confidence, though, and confidence is a key factor in successful hunting.

The same can be said about being prepared during the hunt. Having what we need, when we need it, increases our confidence and performance level. This is why I think my hunting vest is so important. It can serve many purposes for the predator hunter. It

This type of 3-D suit breaks up your profile better than traditional camouflage clothing.

can keep equipment handy, serve as a seat, and hold small game so the hunter's hands remain free. Yes, the vest is a workhorse item, and to my knowledge, there isn't a single one designed specifically for predator hunting. The closest models are made for turkey hunters.

Footwear, like other clothing, should be comfortable. However, I do recommend the use of clean rubber boots or boots with rubber soles, which aid in repelling moisture and help reduce human scent.

Controlling scent is important for most hunting situations, including calling predators. Use scent-free soap and detergent and keep your hunting clothes away from unnatural smells. A lot of hunters even leave their clothing outdoors for a time before a planned hunt to make sure they retain only natural smells found in the woods. Virtually every hunting retailer and catalog now offers a variety of scent- and noise-dampening clothing. These are worth a try, particularly if you're trying to bring in cagey predators.

In subsequent chapters, we'll look at other types of gear, including calls, spotlights, decoys, knives, and more. But my final thought on all types of gear is the simple old Boy Scout motto, "Be prepared."

Chapter
5

SCOUTING

Scouting is without question one of the most important factors in predator-hunting success. The reason for this is simple: you can't shoot something that isn't there. An animal must be within hearing range before it can respond to our calling.

Scouting to me is more than riding around looking for tracks and scat piles. It includes many other elements that hunters sometimes overlook. These things can tell us not only where an animal has been but also where it's going. So I'm always scouting for areas to scout.

Looking for productive hunting lands is a year-round activity. Every time I travel somewhere I'm looking for potential hunting ground. If you wait until a day or two before the season to start your search, you're probably wasting your time.

The first thing to look for is preferred habitat for your target species. For example, bobcats generally prefer dense cover, while red fox like more open terrain. Knowing good habitat includes understanding what various predators like to eat.

Once an area has been selected the next step is to obtain landowner permission. This can often be the most difficult part of the game. Experience has shown me that most landowners don't

Scouting is the fundamental element of successful predator hunting.

care for predators. So if you make a good first impression and make your hunting desires known, you'll have a better chance of gaining access.

Repeat access generally results from our actions while we are on the land. Respect the property and the landowner's wishes at all times, and you may be able to establish a sound, long-term relationship.

Once permission has been secured the next step is to learn everything you can about the property. Start with the landowners. They'll know their property better than anyone else. Ask them to draw a map of the area, detailing boundaries, roads, woodlots, and fields. Now it's time to begin scouting.

Drive or walk access roads to fill in details on the map. Note all geographical features, agricultural croplands, and water sources. These are three critical factors in wildlife habitat. Livestock and

Landowners usually know their property well. Asking them about various features will save you valuable scouting time.

game trails should also be recorded, along with fences, gates, and cattle guards. These travel routes can influence a predator's movements within an area. The same applies to roads, ditches, and dry creekbeds. These are excellent locations for finding good tracking media.

Tracking media is vital for finding an animal's tracks. It consists of any surface that allows an animal's foot to make an impression. Loose dirt, sand, mud, and snow are excellent forms of tracking media. Experienced trackers will never hesitate to use a frost- or dew-covered field when these conditions prevail. The tracks will be gone quickly, but the hunter will have a better handle on how predators and prey use the field.

BECOMING A GOOD SCOUT

Solid scouting skills only come with practice—and more practice. The more efficient we become at reading sign, the better hunters we become. This entails much more than simply looking at an animal's track and saying, "Gee, I guess something was here."

Reading sign is learning to see a track or scat pile and identifying the species immediately. Sign reading means quickly interpreting all the evidence before us. This ability comes from the hunter's knowledge about how pre-existing conditions have affected the evidence.

From the moment it is created, the evidence (track, scat, or urine) of an animal's presence begins to change due to various elements of weather. The time lapse can be determined through the hunter's ability to judge how conditions have changed it. This comes from experience, experience, and more experience. The more we observe how various elements affect a specific type of evidence, the better we become at determining a time lapse. A good way to do this is simply by studying the weather's effect on domestic dog or cat sign, particularly scat piles.

Scat, dung, poop, crap, or whatever you wish to call it, an animal's digestive waste can be very informative to the hunter. Scat tells the hunter an animal has been there, but it also reveals what that animal has been eating. Scat may also indicate other territorial factors such as food caches, den areas, and frequent travel routes. The most successful predator hunters really know their scat.

The appearance of a scat pile will differ between canine (dog) and feline (cat) species. Canine scat generally has a smooth, tubular shape, while feline scat has a rougher, twisted appearance. The size will vary from species to species and from creature to creature due to body size.

Diet and health can also affect the appearance of an animal's scat. Animals of good health, and those feeding on solid food substances, will present a firm tube. Animals of poor health or diet will present a loose form. I've found that animals in the latter category are often less responsive to the ways of the hunter.

Coyote scat next to a three-inch magnum shotshell.

A predator may also use its urine to mark or establish its territory. This can be difficult for the hunter to see unless the urine is located on snow or very dry dirt. In most instances, urine sites are more important to trappers than hunters, but they're still clues to the predator's presence, and often its habits.

THE ALL-IMPORTANT TRACK

The tracks of an animal are probably the most distinctive clue to its presence in an area. To the knowledgeable eye, a track not only identifies the species but also the direction it was traveling at the time of the impression. The track can often inform the hunter of the animal's size and even its sex. That very same track can also reveal the time lapse between creation and discovery.

The track of wild canines—coyotes, red foxes, and wolves—appear more slender in shape than those of domestic dogs and felines. The track of a canine will expose four toes above a triangu-

3–4 in.

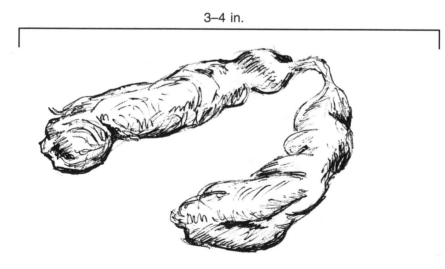

Coyote Scat

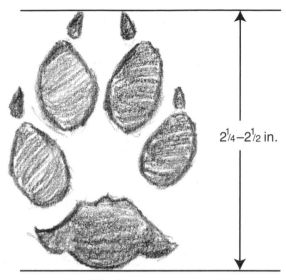

2¼–2½ in.

Hind

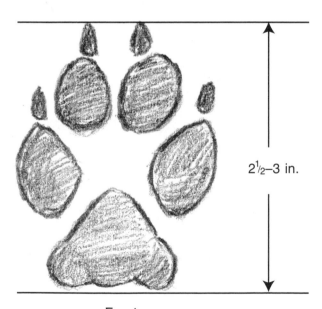

2½–3 in.

Front

Coyote Tracks

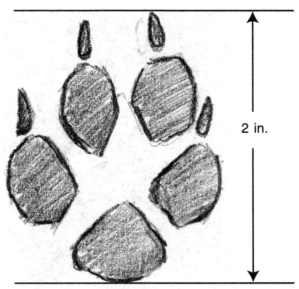

Hind

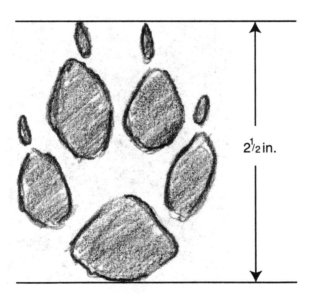

Front

Red Fox Tracks

2–2¹⁄₂ in.

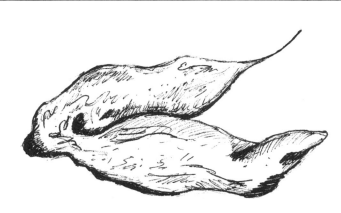

Red Fox Scat

lar-shaped footpad. And the front feet of the canine will be slightly larger than the back, which makes them more effective for digging for food and shelter. In most cases, the tips of the animal's claws can be seen above the toe prints.

The largest North American wild canine is the wolf. Wolf tracks may reach lengths of five inches or more. The length of the coyote's front track will average approximately three inches; a red fox track approximately two inches. The gray fox track averages about one inch less than the red. The track of a gray fox also looks slightly more cat-like.

Feline tracks will also show four toes, but the pad appears much rounder. Generally, the claws will not be apparent. The length of a cougar's track is approximately 3½ to 4 inches. A lynx track generally runs 2¼ to 2½ inches, and a bobcat track around 1¾ to 2 inches.

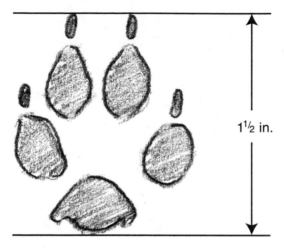

Hind

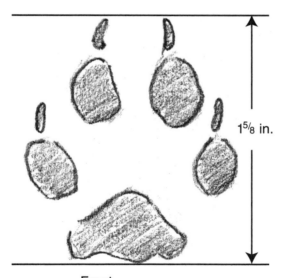

Front

Gray Fox Tracks

2½ in.

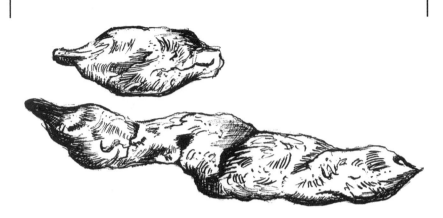

Gray Fox Scat

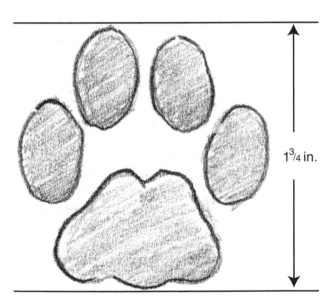

1¾ in.

Hind and Front

Bobcat Track

4 in.

Bobcat Scat

USING TRACKS

The track of an animal is one of the most tattle-telling factors there are. Multiple tracks of a single animal can reveal such things as possible physical characteristics, speed of travel, and possibly even the motivation of the animal. All of these elements can play an important role in successfully hunting the animal.

Decades of tracking have shown me that when tracks appear to veer from a straight line they generally belong to an animal searching for food. In most instances, these tracks will go from one primary prey habitat to another. These are the kind of tracks I like to find. Hungry predators are more likely to relate to, and respond to, the sounds of a caller.

Tracks that form a straight line generally indicate an animal with an agenda. This could be traveling to or from a den site or another designated site. I have located numerous cache sites by following these types of tracks. Hunters may also discover that a straight track line will suddenly change to a winding line. This often means the animal has reached a hunting area. So remember, whatever kind of track line you follow, odds are that you will discover something useful about the animal.

Each animal is an individual and has its own personality. Like humans, some animals simply prefer to do things differently than others. Some are very curious about things, while others are

Clear tracks, like these from a wolf, can tell you much more than just the species of animal. (FWS)

as paranoid as an ant at a cattle farm. One animal might prefer to start walking with the left paw, while the next prefers the right. The personality of an animal can dictate whether it will respond to a caller quickly, cautiously, or not at all. Therefore, I always make note of any suspicions I have about specific animals in an area for future reference.

USING OTHER WILDLIFE

Predator hunters often forget about the feathered predators. Hawks and owls seek many of the same foods as their furry brethren. Rodents, small game, and birds all fall prey to predators. Birds of prey often congregate in areas where food is plentiful, thus informing a hunter about potential hunting grounds. I'm always on the lookout for raptors sitting in trees or on utility lines.

Various other types of birds can lead a predator hunter to promising country. Doves, waterfowl, and even crows will gather in areas that provide abundant food. These foods also attract rodents, which in turn attract predators. Agricultural crops such as wheat, barley, oats, and corn can be very attractive to rodents, birds, and other species of wildlife. This is especially true of corn, which is high in carbohydrates that help generate body heat.

Hunters should always remember that nature has provided all animals with a keen sense of survival. These creatures know exactly what foods can aid them in gaining life-sustaining nutrients. Therefore, many species of prey, especially rodents, seek food sources such as corn when temperatures plummet. Smart hunters know this, and monitor the weather carefully. In most cases, I find that good hunting in such areas begins approximately forty-eight hours before a cold front arrives.

Vultures can also lead a hunter to a potential hunting location. They make their living feeding on the carcasses of the not so fortunate, particularly during big game hunting seasons. Preda-

The tracks of prey animals may lead you to prime predator areas.

tors are often attracted by the presence of these birds, as they know what it means when vultures converge on an area.

USING HUMAN ACTIVITY

Predators can often be located simply by looking at things many people take for granted. One example is how folks dispose of trash; dumpsites are potential sites for locating predators, especially canines. The dumpsite can range from a huge city dump to any location that receives possible predator food on a regular basis.

Prime locations include areas where farmers and ranchers dispose of lost livestock. Coyotes especially will zero in on such an area and use it until the handout has been depleted. In situations like this, establishing an ambush site might be more effective than calling. Carrion feeders tend to be less receptive to calling than animals that have to work for their meals.

Scouting should also include watching for signs of other hunters checking out the same areas you are. This can often become a problem, especially on public hunting lands. Always be on the lookout for signs of human activity (e.g., tire tracks, footprints, spent cartridges). Animals living in areas of high human use have probably been exposed to the ways of the hunter. When possible, reserve these areas for times when other hunters aren't likely to be out and about.

Scouting is as important as being a good marksman. Just like with shooting, it requires the hunter to practice and hone the skill. Scouting is also a great introduction for anyone new to hunting. The hours I have spent scouting with my sons and other youngsters are among the happiest times of my life. Seeing the amazement in those young eyes when I help them discover one of nature's secrets is among the greatest of rewards. So when possible, don't scout alone; a scouting trip could help you find a friend for life.

Open garbage sites often attract predators. Look for sign in the area and then establish calling stands nearby.

Chapter

6

CALLING

To collect fur, you first have to lure it into range and then make the shot count. It's that simple. Knowing how to properly use a caller is critical for success with predators, but techniques for calling, and opinions about calling, vary among hunters. For instance, eastern hunters often claim coyotes are more difficult to call than western hunters.

Having had the pleasure of hunting coyotes all across this great nation, I have formed some of my own opinions about this. The coyote has proven it's one of nature's most adaptable and skillful creatures. It's a pure-blooded survivor, and basically has just one mortal enemy, man. The more encounters an animal survives, the more proficient it becomes at avoiding dangerous situations. And in more populated areas of the East, coyotes are more likely to have had run-ins with humans.

Experience has also led me to believe that some coyotes possess greater learning abilities than others. This has been the focus for numerous research projects conducted by major universities, and many hypotheses have been formed about the coyote's habits and its social functions. So I don't think anyone can determine how hard calling will be based solely on geographical location.

There are simply too many factors that can influence how a coyote might react in a specific calling situation.

Most hunters still believe that good calling leads directly to successful hunting. If no predators were lured in, then there must have been none within listening distance. But does this mean that the key factor in success is merely making noise with a predator caller? Not hardly. In fact, I just view a predator caller as an instrument. Use it well, and good things are more likely to happen, or vice versa.

CALLING PITFALLS

After decades of hunting and calling predators, I am convinced that using a common predator caller is really a double-edged sword. A hunter who knows what he's doing can be a predator's worst nightmare, but in the hands of an incompetent hunter it can quickly educate an animal to avoid all hunters. I have seen the latter happen on many a hunt.

The great Murray Burnham was a pioneer in modern-day predator calling.

It really disgusts me when hunters throw common sense to the wind. A good example of this is how long some people perform the calling sequence. I have watched hunters take a manually operated predator caller (rabbit) and exhale air into it continuously for four to five minutes. Now imagine how this sounds to the ears of a predator well versed in the natural distress sounds of a rabbit. Because a rabbit's lungs are approximately the size of a human thumb, they have a very small capacity in comparison to our own lungs. So such a long calling sequence probably sounds like a 300-pound rabbit to the predator, which is completely unnatural. So the first rule of calling is to do it in a natural manner.

Proper calling presentation, especially with a manual caller, begins with knowledge of the species we are trying to mimic. The volume and length of the calling sequence should carefully mimic likely prey animals. Hunting retailers often carry recordings that make this relatively easy to learn. Nature programs on channels like Animal Planet or the Discovery Channel are also useful for gathering this information.

Another important element in successful calling, especially manual calling, is to be aggressive with the caller. When I say aggressive, I mean calling with enthusiasm. Use your imagination to put yourself in the place of the distressed creature you're trying to imitate. Imagine you're a rabbit hopping along and minding your business, when suddenly the razor-sharp claws of a feral cat grab you and begin tearing you apart. Would you politely go *wee-wee, wee-wee,* or would you scream like bloody hell?

Pain and fear produce emotion, and the sense of an untimely death generally produces a state of extreme excitement, even in a rabbit or rat. This is why the first few seconds of my calling sequence include the loudest and most frantic sounds. Pain, fear, torture, agony—these are the emotions you need to convey in those critical first seconds.

Anyone using a manual caller should know the proper sounds to create before heading afield.

Minimizing movement while calling will improve your score.

Hunters should also avoid a very common mistake when creating these sounds. The mistake I refer to is wriggling your fingers and/or moving your head while calling. I have seen hunters get so caught up with their calling that they start to resemble an Indian snake charmer. Never forget that a pair of super-keen eyes usually accompanies the ears you're playing to.

CREATING THE SEQUENCE

When producing a calling sequence, I start with the frantic notes described above for approximately ten to fifteen seconds. Then I lower the calling volume slightly, while trying to impart a quivering effect in the sounds. My entire calling sequence lasts approximately sixty to ninety seconds, after which I usually remain silent for three minutes or so.

I want any animal that responds to the initial call to continue searching for the source of the distress sounds. In most cases, this means the predator will be moving, which makes it easier for me to detect its presence, as movement catches the eye quicker than a stationary object. By remaining quiet, I can focus on spotting incoming animals.

Always remember to remain as motionless as possible when calling to avoid detection. The finger-wigglers described above must learn to minimize movement. The same is true for hunters that move their heads instead of just their eyes when scanning the cover for a responding animal. Such movements are just habits, and like any habit, they can be broken or corrected through awareness and discipline.

I strongly recommend that you practice your calling routine before ever attempting to lure an actual predator. Practice in front of a video camera or in front of a friend who can point out unconscious movements. Few predators will ever give you a second chance to collect their pelts, so be ready when the first opportunity comes.

SELECTING THE RIGHT CALL

More brands and styles of predator callers are available today than ever before. However, you will quickly discover that most of these callers basically produce the same distress sounds. So is one brand name better than another? Probably, yes. And the reason is the style of the caller.

The mouthpiece and end piece of the caller can affect how well the user is able to manipulate it. If the mouthpiece has a design that is uncomfortable when pressed between the hunter's lips, it'll be more difficult to use. The same goes for the end piece, as this is where the hunter's thumb and index finger circle

Manual callers are now available in a wide range of styles and types.

the caller. If this area is too large, the hunter's hand may become cramped during calling. If it's too small, the hand may cup the caller too tightly, thus restricting the desired sounds. So check out a variety of callers and make sure you end up with the one that's comfortable.

Another important factor I'd consider before buying a manual caller is the degree of volume it generates. Most callers are defined as close-range, medium-range, or long-range. The faintest caller is the squeaker, or coaxer, which produces very faint squeaking sounds much like a rodent or small bird.

Closed-reed calls are probably the easiest type to use. The metal reed in this type of call is located within the body of the call. These calls are inexpensive and allow beginners to master distress sounds without a lot of practice, which is nice when you're just starting out. They also produce a lot of volume.

Open-reed calls have exposed reeds and are usually a bit pricier. They are also more difficult to use effectively. On the other hand, once mastered, they give the caller a wider range of noises to choose from; you're not limited to repeating one identical sound over and over. And they perform well in extremely cold weather.

Squeakers are probably the most overlooked of all predator-calling devices. There are two main types—a rubber-band version and a small bubble containing a tiny reed. The latter type can be attached to the forearm of a rifle or shotgun for easy access during a close-range encounter with a predator. For the most part, I just use my lips to make the squeaking noise that freezes or coaxes animals at very close range. This minimizes any movement that might give me away.

On the other end of the scale, howlers are effective callers for locating coyotes at a distance, as animals tend to respond quickly and loudly to high-volume howls. I sometimes use one on the way to my first calling stand of the day to see if any coyotes are in the area. I mark their locations and pay particular attention to paths they may take to respond to my normal calling sequence. This also helps me figure out how loudly to blow my other calls. It's possible to use howlers to actually bring in coyotes, as well, but they aren't as consistent as other types of calls. This is primarily due to the fact that howls can mean several different things to a coyote. For the most part, they should be used simply to pinpoint coyotes for calling by other methods.

How much overall volume you'll need will be based on the type of terrain you hunt, wind, and noise interference (traffic or planes overhead). One of the most common mistakes novice hunters make is using too much volume. Remember, the hearing capability of a predator is many times greater than our own. In fact, it has been said that a coyote can detect the single squeak of a field mouse at over seventy-five yards on a calm day. That's something

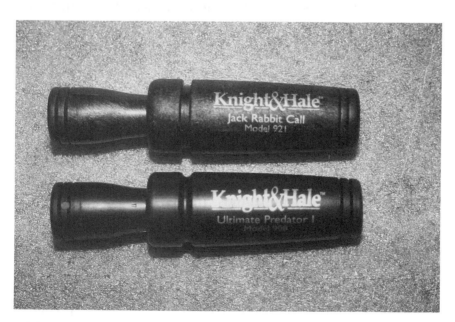

Knight & Hale is one of the leading makers of game calls.

you might want to keep in mind before you split your buddy's eardrums with that long-range caller on your next hunting trip.

RINGING THE DINNER BELL

Selecting the proper sound may become frustrating for hunters new to the predator game. The wide variety of calling sounds now on the market doesn't make this any easier, particularly when it comes to electronic game callers.

What is the best sound, or sounds, to use if you want to call a coyote? Should it be a distressed jackrabbit or the bleating of a deer fawn? In the end, hunters probably spend too much time worrying about the perfect sound instead of focusing on other elements. But there's little doubt in my mind that the sound of a distressed rabbit has lured in more predators than any other sound. So is this the only sound we need? Not hardly, and here's why.

Most predator hunters today are heading afield with distressed rabbit callers. The more animals hear this sound, the more likely they are to become accustomed to it. These predators are often referred to as "call shy." In fact, I have actually witnessed coyotes run away when they hear these sounds. They had somehow learned that the sound meant danger. So using only distressed rabbit sounds isn't enough; I always carry an assortment of sounds with me and try to assess the given conditions before choosing one.

If I'm hunting in an area I think has received much calling pressure, I avoid standard sounds. Instead, I'll use a sound that might be fresh, such as a distressed chicken or puppy. Both sounds create the impression that something is hurt and is an easy meal for a hungry predator.

I am also a firm believer that individual predators prefer certain sounds to others. This is especially true of smaller predators like raccoons and foxes. These animals tend to focus more on the

Distressed rabbit sounds are the most popular for calling coyotes, but in some areas it pays to experiment with other sounds.

lesser prey species, such as birds and rodents, particularly in areas where larger predators are also present. Small predators know they can become prey themselves and generally avoid anything that might also seem particularly attractive to the big boys.

Making good judgments about what call to use when can only come from experience. So watch and listen, and don't be afraid to experiment.

MECHANICAL MARVELS

Electronic game-calling machines make calling game as simple as pushing a button or flipping a switch. These machines have transformed tone-deaf sportsmen into expert predator callers, and they're an integral part of the modern caller's arsenal.

The electronic caller first came on the scene in the mid-1960s. Early names found on these devices included Bounty

Hunter, Johnny Stewart, and Burnham Brothers. These units were basically battery-powered record players. And the records had an average playing time of around twenty minutes. When the recording stopped, the needle would have to be reset before calling could resume. This was very frustrating for the hunter whose record stopped just as a predator appeared.

Today's electronic callers are much more convenient to use. They are powered by rechargeable batteries, and the sounds are of much higher quality and recorded on cassette or CD. However, I don't like the fact that most recordings are continuous playing. All of my modern electronic callers are equipped with remote-control units, which allow me to control every element of the calling sequence with the touch of a button. Remote-control units also allow the hunter to place the sound source away from

Electronic callers like the FoxPro have made calling as easy as it gets.

his shooting position, thus reducing the chances of being spotted by a responding animal.

The only negative factor associated with these models is cost. Electronic units generally range from a hundred dollars to several hundred, depending on the brand, type, and options.

The real value of these machines is in producing sounds that are difficult, if not impossible, to mimic with a manual caller. Being able to use such sounds gives the modern hunter a great advantage.

CALLING TECHNIQUES

The most vital element of any calling technique is what I've stressed throughout this chapter—keeping it natural. The more naturally we relay our message to the predator, the less reason it has to be suspicious.

But experience has taught me that there's no such thing as a single perfect calling technique. Developing proper calling techniques takes versatility and personal experience. Sure, my standard technique of one minute of calling followed by two or three minutes of silence has sent scores of critters to their maker, but there have been many times where I think trying something a little different would have added to my success. Be ready to experiment anytime you are calling in an area that gets much hunting pressure.

The most common alteration I make in my standard technique is decreasing the length of the calling sequence. Instead of calling for sixty seconds or more, I'll drop it to around fifteen seconds. I still allow a time lapse of a couple of minutes, and then resume calling with lower volume on the next round. In most cases, I limit my calling time with this technique to around twenty minutes per stand. If the decreasing volume hasn't drawn the critter in by then, staying with it probably won't help.

The best camouflage in the world won't help if your calling doesn't sound natural.

THE RIGHT CALLING LOCATION

The location hunters call from is as important as the call used. The location, or stand site, as it's often referred to, is the spot where everything about the hunt must come together. If there is some sort of flaw in the stand site, the hunter usually goes home empty-handed. I've been there plenty of times myself, and the culprit is often simple neglect. Neglecting to pay attention to my surroundings. Neglecting to be careful in the habitat of a keen and cautious animal. In short, I stopped paying attention to details and started relying on lady luck for success.

Experience is always the best teacher when it comes to selecting a calling site, although there are a few general factors to consider. One is wind direction. Hunters must always respect the olfactory capabilities of predators. These animals can detect human scent from great distances in the slightest breeze. Try to move, and call, into the wind whenever possible.

Visibility is another key factor. The sight lines the location provides usually determine how quickly the hunter can detect a responding animal, which in turn dictates the amount of time the hunter has to prepare for a shot. And more time often equates to greater success.

Concealment plays a role, too. Hunters often seek areas that provide plenty of visibility but fail to notice that they themselves are too exposed. The stand site should always provide the hunter with at least enough concealment to distort his outline while calling. I also search for stand sites that offer concealment while I'm entering and exiting the location. Animals in the area may wonder about the sounds they're hearing, but without visual confirmation they might not be immediately spooked.

It pays to have a variety of possible stand sites scouted out well before a planned hunt, so you can choose the best based on

Good calling locations provide visibility and concealment for the hunter.

prevailing conditions. The distances between stand sites will vary depending on terrain and cover, but will normally range from half a mile to a mile or so.

Experienced hunters usually return to stand sites that have been productive in past seasons. I have some locations that have produced year after year for as long as I can remember. These areas usually have some special habitat features that concentrate prey animals.

In open country, the hunter must take advantage of any available cover.

An excellent example of this is one of my favorite bobcat hunting areas, which I use during extremely dry conditions. It includes a shallow beaver pond set in the middle of some heavy brush country. In fact, the undergrowth is so thick that I have to use the streambed to gain access to the beaver pond. Visibility is nil until you reach the pond. In a dry year, this pond holds most of the available water in the area, which draws in a variety of prey, creating a prime feeding area for predators. The number of bobcats I've collected from this area escapes my memory, but I didn't nickname it the "Litter Box" for nothing.

No matter what caller, technique, or stand you choose, you must call with confidence. This feeling comes from scouting, practice, and experience, and it can have a very positive impact on your days afield. Confidence leads to success and success makes your hunting experiences more enjoyable. And isn't that the point of it all?

Chapter
7

HUNTING THE COYOTE

The coyote is one of nature's most amazing creatures. A master survivor, it has expanded its range like few other animals across North America. Today, the coyote sings its nightly songs from the Atlantic to the Pacific.

Unlike many predators, the coyote has adapted well to the incursions of civilization, even surviving deliberate campaigns to exterminate it in many regions. It's been trapped. Its young have been robbed from dens and slaughtered. It's been shot on sight whenever possible from land, and even from the air. Chemical warfare also inflicted heavy losses to the coyote population. Poisons such as strychnine, arsenic, and the ever-so-lethal Compound 1080 were used.

Yet the coyote weathered all these storms and continued to flourish. I firmly believe that if the world ever ends, the coyote, crow, and cockroach will find a way to dance on our bones.

Entire volumes have been written about the coyote. But without a doctorate in biology, most of these studies are of little value to the hunter. However, there are some basic biological factors I believe every coyote hunter should be aware of.

KNOW YOUR PREY

The coyote (*Canis latrans*) is a North American mammal that resembles many types of Old World jackals. In fact, the coyote was frequently referred to as the American jackal by early explorers. Some people speculate that the modern coyote originated from wild canids that survived persecution by humans during the early settlement of this country. This may very well be accurate, as coyotes commonly found in the north (*Canis latrans thamnos*) resemble the gray wolf. This species generally has a grayish pelt with a darker gray or black back.

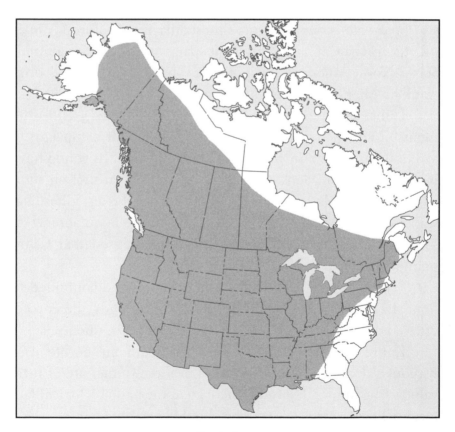

Coyote Range

Geographic location influences both color and size. Males and females in Iowa average thirty and twenty-five pounds respectively, and usually appear rather shaggy. But coyotes in the Northeast average thirty-seven and thirty-two pounds respectively, and present heavier coats. All coyotes have slender proportions, including a long, narrow, pointed nose, large pointed ears, slender legs, small feet, and a bushy tail.

The southern and western coyote (*Canis latrans frustror*) resembles the red wolf, which was once common across America's prairie lands. This is the most abundant subspecies, as it includes the common coyote of the West. These animals generally present a light gray and red pelt with darker backs of black or reddish-brown. Like their northern cousins, the average weights vary from region to region. Males and females average twenty-four and nineteen pounds in Texas and twenty-eight and twenty-three

The coyote has thrived despite extermination efforts and shifting environments.

pounds in Tennessee. Like most North American mammals, the farther north they live, the larger they are.

Coyotes may mate for life and usually breed during February and March, depending on the region. The gestation period lasts for approximately sixty-three days and yields around five to seven pups. These are usually raised in earthen dens, but logs, abandoned buildings, and other dwellings may be used, as multiple dens are not uncommon.

During the first four to six weeks of life, nourishment is obtained solely from the mother's milk. Then the parents will feed their young by regurgitating food they have gathered elsewhere. This usually consists of insects and small mammals, along with vegetation and even carrion.

Within days of their birth, the young are taught to hunt. This starts with capturing insects. In time, the pups will gain the skills necessary to stalk rodents and other small creatures. They continue to grow and learn throughout the summer. In some areas of the country young males will have already reached twenty pounds or more, with females averaging five to ten pounds less.

Due to their expanding range over recent decades, variations in body size and habits have occurred. While this may not interest some people, serious hunters should take note. Eastern coyotes often must be hunted differently than their western counterparts, because the habitats and food sources are different.

NEW HORIZONS

The mighty Mississippi River is located approximately one hour's drive from my home. As a youngster I dreamed of going west to hunt coyotes as they didn't exist east of the river, or at least that's what most folks thought during the middle and late 1960s. Never did I dream that my first coyote would come from within a mile

Geography can have an effect on body size and specific habits.

of my home in Tennessee. I also never imagined that the coyote would influence my life as it has.

Eastern colonization of the coyote occurred during two different time periods. The first movement (northern front) began during the early 1900s when coyotes from Minnesota, Wisconsin, and Manitoba moved eastward into Ontario and Michigan. By the 1930s, the coyote was singing its songs in New York, and it continued to expand its range. By the 1950s coyotes were roaming throughout New England and south into Pennsylvania.

The second movement (southern front) began much later. Coyotes moved from Texas and Oklahoma into Arkansas and Louisiana during the 1940s and '50s. Pressure from extermination efforts in the West probably caused this movement.

The main thrust of this movement took the coyote across the Mississippi River by the early 1960s. It is assumed that they walked across the frozen river during particularly cold periods.

The eastward expansion of the coyote has provided hunters with a wealth of new opportunities.

Numerous bridges were also constructed over the Mississippi River during this era, providing easy access for coyotes seeking new hunting grounds.

There is also some documentation for coyotes being transported across the Mississippi River before the major migration. They were primarily released for sport, to be run down by hounds. Animals that escaped the chase were free to roam about and mate, thus laying the groundwork for new populations.

However the coyote got its start in the East, one thing quickly became clear: It was there to stay.

THE GOOD, THE BAD, AND THE ALMOST ALWAYS UGLY

Like most predators, coyotes are seen as both good and bad. For example, if a rancher sees a coyote eating a rat near his grainfield, he might label it a good coyote. But if the same coyote is spotted chewing on a lamb or calf the next day, well, now it's a bad coyote.

Hunters, like farmers and ranchers, usually hold a grudge against the coyote due to its appetite for game animals. Rabbit and upland bird hunters, in particular, tend to feel this way. Anyone who takes the time to examine coyote scat within an area will generally discover the reason for a decline in the local rabbit population.

Deer hunters also lose potential trophies each year due to the coyote's hunger for meat. Research papers on deer populations almost always include the coyote as a factor in fawn mortality. These scientific papers generally note that coyotes account for only a small percentage of deaths, and I certainly can't dispute these findings. However, for decades I have been a keen observer of coyote scat, and during the periods of annual fawn birthing I have found numerous scat piles full of fawn hair.

My observations (again, county-boy style) have also indicated a substantial decline in the number of twin fawn sightings

The coyote's bad reputation among ranchers and big game hunters has led to easier access to private lands for many predator hunters.

Coyotes are smart and adapt well to whatever food sources present themselves, which means that everything from songbirds to deer is fair game.

during the primary birthing periods. In fact, the ratio of no fawn per doe has increased within my area over the past decade or so. Of course, other factors of mortality exist—disease, starvation, illegal harvest, automobiles—but this decline has become more apparent since the number of predators has increased. I don't think a master's degree is required to correctly assess what's happening within the environment.

A TRULY ASTONISHING CREATURE

I have always prided myself on being a student of nature, and studying coyotes over the years has taught me quite a bit. I have held off shooting at the last minute on countless occasions just because I sensed the coyote was about to show me something new; something that would make me more productive as a hunter or trapper.

An excellent example of this occurred several years ago. I was driving along a major road and happened to notice a coyote sitting in a nearby field. I was immediately curious about its behavior. In minutes, I had turned the truck around and parked on the side of the road and was spying on it through my binoculars. The coyote continued to simply sit there staring across the field, and after following the direction of its gaze, I discovered that it was watching a house cat.

I could just make out the Persian cat crouching low in the grass. The cat was still as a rock, returning the coyote's stare across about seventy-five yards of real estate. It wasn't until the coyote got up, moved a few yards towards the cat, and sat back down that I noticed the second coyote.

It was located approximately fifty yards behind the cat, in a low crouching position. Things were getting interesting. The second coyote never made a move until the first one did. As before, the first coyote continued to take only a few steps before sitting down. A couple of times, the first coyote even stopped to scratch its ear with its hind foot. Whenever these actions occurred, the second coyote used the opportunity to close the gap on the cat.

The game continued for close to half an hour, with both coyotes gaining ground on the cat. Then, as if a silent command had been given, the first coyote suddenly stood up and began wailing directly at the cat. Naturally, this alarmed the Persian. It lost no time in scurrying in the opposite direction — right into the waiting jaws of the second coyote. The poor cat never had a chance of escaping the dynamic duo. But the show was still far from over.

The first coyote began trotting toward the prize, but something didn't look right. I noticed it was limping, not allowing its right hind foot to touch the ground. I then watched in amazement as the second coyote surrendered the cat to the cripple. It took just a few minutes for it to devour about half the cat, while the second coyote watched and waited a few yards away.

Suddenly the first coyote stopped eating. It limped a few yards away and laid down. The second coyote quickly jumped up and consumed the rest of the meal. As I was already quite late for an appointment, I left both coyotes lying contentedly in the field.

There was no question the coyotes had worked as a team. The first coyote had served as a decoy to keep the cat's attention directed away from its partner. Had the coyotes somehow planned their actions in advance? If so, had they communicated vocally to force the cat to take refuge in the open field? I was sorry I had missed the start of the episode, as I could now only speculate about the answers to these questions.

Then there is the manner of how they shared their catch. This really astonished me, as the second coyote was of greater size than the first. It could have easily taken the entire meal for itself if it wanted to. Certainly, there are still things to be learned about the coyote's intelligence and social behavior. Maybe some of the Indian legends are correct and the coyote actually does possess magical powers.

The only thing I am sure about is that the coyote is a remarkable creature.

Chapter

8

EARLY ENCOUNTERS WITH COYOTES

The decade of the 1970s was one of great change for me. For one thing, I started my first full-time job. Unlike some, I found the second shift (3–11 PM) perfect for my lifestyle. I could hunt or fish most of the day and still keep a job that supported my daily habits. The only real frustrations I had were overtime at work and the coyote. Members of the opposite sex were still viewed as a costly hindrance most of the time.

Coyotes were migrating eastward at a steady pace from neighboring Missouri. More and more reports of coyote sightings were reaching me daily. Deer, ducks, and other game were becoming secondary interests as my passion grew for hunting the coyote. The only problem was that I was doing a lot of hunting and very little killing.

I read everything I could find pertaining to coyotes and hunting them. I spent hours after work riding the countryside and listening for the coyote's howl. If luck prevailed and I homed in on one, I'd be out at dawn in hot pursuit. In most cases, my only rewards were lost sleep and a half-frozen butt. Occasionally, I would catch a glimpse of something I thought was a coyote, or hear the barking of something I knew was a coyote. Either way, I went home frustrated as hell.

GOMER PREVAILS

The antics of television's Gomer Pyle sparked a new nickname for anyone committing a half-witted act. Therefore, my friends were quick to apply the label to me for neglecting a buddy's sister. She was a gorgeous brunette with a wonderful personality, but I was saving up for a new rifle, electronic game caller, and other essentials.

Besides, I thought everyone knew that the life of a hunter was a lonely one. After much harassment, I finally invited her on a date, which consisted of a few hamburgers, a twelve-pack of Bud, and riding around listening to my eight-track tape player. My entire collection of tunes consisted of two Waylon Jennings tapes, Creedence Clearwater Revival, and Conway Twitty. Occasionally, the music would be paused so we could look at the lovely stars above in silence. During these romantic moments she would smile at me in the moonlight while I analyzed the nightly sounds around us. She seemed to be having a good time until I detected the faint yelping of—you guessed it—coyotes.

I was quickly speeding along the gravel roads. The date had been fine, but now I had to locate the animals' exact position. Needless to say, our first (and last) date was cut short. Dawn was only hours away, and I had a lot of preparations to make.

The following morning was an experience I'll never forget. The sounds of my calling echoed across the land in the dim light of dawn, and I clenched my rifle tensely. Only the nip of the cold autumn air disrupted my thoughts as I scanned the harvested cornfield in front of me. Then, without giving any indication of its approach, a coyote appeared at the edge of the field.

Standing like a statue, the coyote stared in my direction. Golden sunlight glistened from its fur as I slowly readied the rifle.

Tension blended with excitement, causing my hands to tremble. I could feel my heart pounding in my ears while I centered the scope on the coyote's chest. As if it had been given a silent command, the coyote began loping toward me.

Several seconds passed while I watched the advancing animal through the scope. Only the click of the rifle's safety being released disturbed the silence. My finger tightened on the trigger, and the coyote crumbled in its tracks. My proud moment was interrupted by the sight of three other coyotes racing from the field. I grabbed my caller and quickly repeated the bunny blues, hoping that somehow the coyotes would turn back. They were long gone, of course, but I did get one coyote, and it was time to show it off to all my friends.

GOMER GRADUATES

The majority of my friends sided with the pretty brunette, but a few of my hardcore hunting buddies understood the importance of the situation. And the next morning one of the "true" friends accompanied me on the hunt.

We positioned ourselves downwind of the same cornfield. I wasn't sure about how smart it was to repeat the same setup as the day before, but we were encouraged by the abundance of coyote tracks and my earlier success. We had also brainstormed the idea of using multiple calls, which we felt would double our odds for success.

Soon, our callers were blaring in the dawning light. We called for several minutes before I detected some frantic whispering from my partner, which I instantly interpreted as "I see one!" I spun my head around in time to see him pointing his deer rifle. I scrambled to do the same as two charging coyotes broke off their advance.

Without thought, we both zeroed in on the same coyote. Then an ear-shattering blast occurred as his .30–06 and my 6mm

Famous game-call maker Harold Knight was one of my first hunting partners. Success like this came few and far between in our early days together.

Remington exploded simultaneously. This resulted in one very dead coyote. We quickly turned our attention to the other coyote.

Shot after shot pounded the frosty cornfield until our chambers were empty. Astonished at what we had done, we sat in total amazement as the last echoes died. I just couldn't accept the fact that we had both shot the same coyote—and let the other escape. My partner could only mutter to himself as we went to retrieve what was left of the coyote.

An examination of the remains proved that it was a youngster, just like mine from the previous day. Pulling a Lucky Strike from its package, I began to think about the coyotes I'd seen on the first hunt. All had been approximately the same size, so it made sense to assume that we had called in the same group of animals, a pack of yearlings.

Three more trips over the course of the next week yielded nothing. There were still plenty of tracks, but I think the coyotes had figured out the true meaning of the distressed bunny sounds. But if one pack proved so responsive initially, why wouldn't another?

I redoubled my efforts, spending even more time riding and listening for coyotes after work. This paid off, as I located a few more groups that soon brought my kill tally into the double digits. I was now learning a lot about the coyote and its habits— things I hadn't read about in magazines, but that came through my own trial and error.

HARD KNOCKS

The latter part of the seventies found me viewing things from a totally different perspective. The freedoms of bachelorhood were only fond memories, and I was struggling with the pressures of family life. Kids, bills, layoffs, and a nagging wife (now an ex-nagging wife) gave the word "struggle" a whole new meaning. I tackled any job that could provide an extra dollar. Part-time carpentry, farming, and woodcutting filled the gaps during the summer. Winter income was supplemented by collecting fur with both gun and traps. Wild fur prices were at an all-time high. A nice bobcat or a couple of prime red fox equaled more money than a week in the factory; not so with the eastern coyote.

Coyote pelts from my region were of little value. In fact, the coyote was costing me more money than it was worth. Those devils were taking one to three foxes from my traps each week. This was nothing short of a declaration of war, as times were tough. Little did I know what kind of adversary the coyote would prove to be.

My determination grew each time a coyote escaped my steel. I tested theory after theory as I tried to gain the upper hand. Then, after a long month of defeats, I began thinking like a predator, respecting the coyote as I never had before.

I started by using a larger trap, usually a No. 2. Naturally, I constructed the trap site as I would for a fox. This is commonly referred to as a "dirt hole set." Instead of using a fox lure, I substi-

During the late 1970s, prime red fox pelts were worth a lot of money.

tuted a squirt of coyote urine. To my surprise, I still took only a few coyotes, and my fox profits continued to decline. However, I was learning more and more about the animal's habits, and my respect was bordering on pure hatred.

CRACKING THE ICE

The first big break I received in my personal war occurred one very cold night. I had finished my shift at the factory and decided to check a few traps on the way home. The ground was covered in a heavy frost and the moon was full. It was almost like walking in daylight as I strolled along the trap line.

I had just recovered a nice male mink from a set I had made at the edge of a creek when I heard the echo of a lone fox barking. I hurried toward the sound, as I knew I had placed a trap in the vicinity. Suddenly, it sounded as if the fox had fallen into a blender. Screams of pain echoed through the woods for several minutes before a deafening silence prevailed. Then the echo of a lone coyote's bark filled the cold air, sending a chill right through me.

I began carefully stalking the location, armed with only a .22 pistol. All I could think of was closing the gap and punching a hole in that damned dog. Hate dominated my every thought as I slowly closed the distance.

I detected the dark silhouettes of two coyotes crossing the adjoining field. But, needless to say, by the time I completed the stalk the culprits had vanished. Only the tattered, blood-soaked remains of the fox greeted me at the trap site. I cursed to myself while gathering the remains, taking some solace in knowing the coyotes would be deprived of this easy meal.

The following morning, I learned that another prime fox had been stolen from my line. But this time the culprit proved to have two feet instead of four. I was already too focused on my four-footed foe to worry about anything else at the moment, though, so later that day I took up a position inside a fencerow approximately a quarter-mile from where the coyotes had last attacked. Approximately twenty yards away, I had formed one of my prized pelts into a decoy. I settled in and then put my Johnny Stewart electronic caller to use playing a fox-in-distress call.

I clinched the rifle as the minutes ticked by. Only the sounds of the caller disturbed the countryside in the fading light of day. Suddenly, I detected movement across the field. I slowly raised the rifle to use the scope for target identification, and saw a pair of pointed ears signaling that a coyote was about to make its move.

I watched with joy as the coyote continued its advance. And I could see the animal was completely focused on the decoy. It slowed to a trot. Then, without any apparent provocation, the animal did something that astonished me.

The coyote suddenly stopped. Long moments passed as I watched it stand and stare at the fox pelt. Its stone-like posture was broken only by a slight side-to-side movement of its head. Then the coyote raised its head toward the sky and produced a single long and mournful howl.

Stunned, I continued to peer over the top of the scope, waiting for other coyotes to join the one before me. The animal suddenly turned and stared directly at me, as if it somehow knew what was coming.

Finally, the animal lowered its head and began to slowly walk away. It carefully placed one paw in front of the other while holding its tail in a submissive posture. I became even more convinced that it knew it was about to enter the hereafter. Within minutes of pulling the trigger, I heard a distant lone howl that made me wonder if it wasn't a way of saying goodbye.

I would later hear this howl many times in many places all across the country as I continued to pursue coyotes. I have come to think of it as some kind of death chant.

Chapter

9

WESTERN COYOTES

Hunting the lands west of the Mississippi had long been a dream of mine. The countless articles I'd read had me foolishly believing many things. I was actually more worried about running out of ammunition than using it. My impression was that a predator was peeking around every cactus, and all I had to do was show up and shoot it.

My first western hunting adventure finally came during the mid-1980s. The destination was the cactus-covered lands of southern Texas. Here, I would hook up with a well-known game-call manufacturer and an outdoor journalist. The goal was to pile up stacks of coyote carcasses while gathering material for future magazine articles.

It was late February and the weather had turned warm. The first animal I encountered was an extremely large rattlesnake fresh from its den. This meeting quickly showed my companions I was either a real tinhorn or a borderline idiot. Either way, the big buzztail was later skinned, tanned, and mounted on my office wall.

We hunted hard for two days and part of one night. I was lucky enough to collect a nice bobcat and one coyote, and I

The author with his first western coyote.

worked in another pack of four coyotes that managed to escape unharmed. From one companion, I heard a lot of reasons why the animals were not responding, but the other became a dear friend.

My dreams of finding big numbers in the Promised Land were dampened, but the thrill of hunting this land captivated me.

LOVING THE LONE STAR STATE

Two years would pass before I had a chance to return to Texas, but in the meantime I was able to hunt in California, Kansas, Idaho, and Colorado. All of these states produced some excellent hunts, and I was enjoying my adventures. Then I received an invitation to hunt south Texas with another game-call manufacturer. The hunt was to last for three or four days, and would again take place during mid-February.

My host picked me up at the San Antonio airport and we drove several hours farther south. Darkness had fallen by the time we arrived at our destination, and my companion wasted no time in rigging spotlights. We had come to hunt, and that was what we were going to do.

Soon the headlights of the pickup were knifing through the darkness, exposing a vast sea of prickly pear. Dust bellowed from beneath the tires as we followed the dirt trail, which the locals called a *sendero*. We finally halted at the intersection of two trails. Here, I would quickly learn that my host was playing for keeps.

I took my place inside a specially built platform fitted into the bed of the truck, called a "varmint rack," and was given my instructions. Like my partner, I held a rifle and a spotlight with a red lens. If I spotted the shining eyes of a predator I would hold the light while my companion used the gun. The role would be reversed if he spotted the critter.

Eastern hunters venturing to the West should bring realistic expectations.

I can't recall if we scored on that particular stand, but I do remember collecting several predators that night and hunting past sunrise before returning to camp. This would be the routine for the entire hunt, as only eating and sleeping interfered with hunting. This was more of what I had in mind when I thought about the hunting lands of my dreams.

I returned to hunt this area many times with my companion in the next few years. South Texas had its good and bad days, as did Wyoming, Arizona, New Mexico, and all the other states I ventured to. I learned that every location was different, and the animals reacted differently, as well. There were no more guarantees in these places than there had been on my home ground. This was especially true when the critters were subjected to what I can only define as "supreme stupidity."

THE MASTERMIND

One of the perks of my line of work is that I get hunting invitations from almost every point of the compass. A red flag goes up immediately on some of these proposed hunts, a feeling I get simply by listening to the person giving the invite. However, this was not the case with a gentleman I'll call Fred.

I met Fred at a hunting show and read some of the brochures for his guide service. His photo album contained some impressive whitetail deer and several piles of deceased coyotes. It seemed like good evidence of the success of his guide service, so I accepted his offer to hunt.

Months went by, and at last it was time for our hunt. I flew several hours to the west, and Fred greeted me at the airport. My enthusiasm was running high, and I was hoping to use a lot of ammunition. Fred also seemed to be excited as he told me about all the potential targets he had been seeing. In fact, Fred seemed a little too excited.

That night at dinner we elected to make deer our primary objective and then go to work on the coyotes. Fred informed me that he had a monster buck located and felt confident we could get it in a day's time. This made me question Fred and his methods, but I kept it to myself.

The following day we met the dawn sitting side by side in the back of Fred's pickup truck. Here we scanned the prickly pear and cactus, hoping to see Fred's monster buck. As we moved our binoculars across the horizon, I wondered what Fred's plan was going to be if we saw it. The terrain was fairly open, and the thorn-covered vegetation would make stalking difficult.

Approximately an hour of driving and glassing had passed when I detected a glimmer of sunlight reflecting off polished antlers. In seconds, the head of the deer appeared over the prickly pear, a small eight-point rack. I focused in behind the little buck, figuring Fred's monster buck might be following.

"There he is," barked Fred, as I began franticly searching in all directions. "There, to your right!" commanded my companion, as the little buck reappeared in the binoculars. Again I scanned all around the little buck, searching for another one. Then it dawned on me; I was already looking at Fred's "monster" buck.

I was in a pickle, as I most certainly did not want to insult my host, or his definition of a monster buck. However, I didn't have the slightest desire to tag the deer I was looking at.

Fred was now whispering to me in a commanding voice to shoot the little buck. I pondered my next move. The idiot buck stood stock still, staring in our direction. Then I had an idea that would save the deer and my self-respect. I simply launched the bullet inches over the deer's back, and it scurried safely into the dense cover.

The look on Fred's face was not a happy one. He sensed what I had done, but never said a word. I tried to act disappointed and cheerfully suggested we forget about deer and start on the coyotes. He readily agreed, as he knew his buck would really be hard to hunt now that I'd put it on notice.

We spent the next two days chasing predators, but this also became a fiasco due to Fred's hunting techniques. In fact, it was a complete joke; only a single gray fox was fooled. The really sad thing was that I learned the photos I had seen were actually from Fred's buddies, who allowed him to use their images for his brochure.

To say the least, such a lack of professionalism infuriated me. Fred never received my support for his guide operation. His ideas about a good guide service were far different from mine.

GREAT GUIDES

Hunters venturing to unfamiliar territory should seek the assistance of a reputable guide. This can eliminate a lot of potential problems and increase the odds for experiencing a good hunt.

A really good guide is worth every penny of his wages. In fact, a good guide might even save you money. How can this be possible, you ask? Simple. Don't view the guide as a magic genie who somehow conjures up game for you to shoot. Look at the guide as a teacher. Study his methods and techniques, and you'll come away with a distilled version of his experience in the field. Information and skills you'll likely be able to apply to a variety of future hunting situations.

A reputable guide or outfitter is just like you, a sportsman. But he has taken his passion for the sport and turned it into a profession. A good guide is under constant pressure to produce for the client. He must cope with the elements and use his skills like a surgeon uses a scalpel. If not, he's out of business or soon will be. This is why it is so important to check out a potential guide or outfitter before plunking down your money.

New styles of camouflage have allowed predator hunters more options for staying hidden in the field.

Of course, the bobcat's natural camouflage is tough to beat.

The amazingly adaptable coyote continues to expand its range. It can now be hunted from coast to coast. (Sue Weddle)

Electronic callers easily duplicate natural distress sounds, leaving hunters free to concentrate on their shooting.

This hunter is about to score on a bobcat, one of nature's most elusive predators.

In the hands of an expert, manual callers can be deadly on coyotes..

In many parts of the East, the red fox has been forced to adapt to burgeoning coyote populations. (Sue Weddle)

Due to the sport's growing popularity, manufacturers are now making rifles and cartridges specifically for predator hunters.

Shotguns are a good choice for close-range shooting and offer fast follow-up shots.

Scouting thoroughly and establishing good stand sites in advance of the hunt will pay big dividends.

Ranchers are usually happy to allow hunters access to their land when coyotes are the target. (Joe Arterburn)

In many areas across North America it's possible to take coyotes and bobcats from the same location.

Long the nemesis of farmers everywhere, foxes have also learned that suburban areas can provide new sources of food.

Hunting with a partner is a very effective way to take predators, as the extra pair of eyes helps spot animals responding to the caller.

Mountain lions feed primarily by stalking deer but will sometimes respond to predator callers. Just be ready when they do . . .

Like all major predators, bears will often investigate animal-in-distress sounds. Here legendary call-maker Murray Burnham poses with a fine color-phase bear. (Jim Zumbo)

The bobcat is an efficient predator, which doesn't endear it to hunters who like to pursue birds and other small game. (Sue Weddle)

Bringing in that first coyote of the day always gives the hunter a boost in confidence.

A good guide can mean the difference between success and failure when you're hunting in unfamiliar country.

Start with the guide's reputation. This reputation is his professional lifeline, and he knows it. Reputable guides are always in demand and generally have a waiting list. The only exception to this is a guide who works on a first-come, first-served basis. So before even contacting a potential guide, review magazine articles, ads, and other resources that might validate his standing. Once you're satisfied on this score, it's time to invest in a phone call.

Inform the guide of your desires and timeframe you have available for hunting so you can learn right off the bat whether things will match up. Find out what realistic expectations would be for the hunt, as a good guide will always be truthful about this. And don't divert from the purpose of your call. These people are conducting a business and are usually quite busy.

The hunter should also seek the guide's advice about equipment. Remember, this is a person who copes with the given hunting conditions every day, and he usually knows what works best. Inquire about the average number of hunters he has served during the past few seasons. Don't be shy about asking his percentage of repeat business, and always ask for references. Then check in with a few of his out-of-state references, if available. If the guide can't provide references, start looking for someone else.

WESTERN WONDERLANDS

Experience has shown me that there are a lot of great hunting opportunities in the West. Some, in my opinion, are better than others for one reason or another, but what suits my fancy might not work for the next guy. Some hunters might not like hunting in the warmer temperatures of southern Arizona, while others might love it. This is one of the things that makes this country so great; there is something for everyone.

Western hunting lands include a wide variety of climates and terrain.

Some of the best western predator hunting I've experienced has occurred in places not often referred to as predator hotspots. A piece of public hunting land in the state of Missouri was one such place. It was here that a friend and I experienced some of the fastest coyote shooting I have ever had in a single day. And we'd actually come to hunt waterfowl, not coyotes. So the coyotes we collected were whacked at close range with steel shot, if that provides any indication about how good it really was.

I have had similar experiences while pursuing western big game. In fact, I once gave up on an antelope hunt and spent three days blasting coyotes, which greatly pleased my rancher/host. He was so happy that I now have an open invitation to hunt antelope and mule deer whenever I want, so long as I don't forget the coyotes.

So if you want to hunt somewhere in the West, there are plenty of places to go. The key is to do a little research and decide what you want to hunt and where you want to do it. Predators in the Southwest are usually very abundant, while their northern, or higher altitude, cousins make extremely beautiful trophies.

Chapter
10

THINKING DIFFERENTLY FOR EASTERN PREDATORS

The geographical region you hunt should dictate the manner in which you hunt. In a sense, geography is simply another word for habitat. The habitat an animal resides in generally influences its habits. Therefore, analyzing the habitat of a specific animal is a key factor in successful hunting, particularly when it comes to eastern coyotes.

Unlike some coyote-hunting gurus, I do not believe a coyote is a coyote anywhere it is found. I have hunted this animal all across the United States and in parts of Canada, and sometimes the hunting was easy, sometimes not. In most cases, the tough spots were affected by human activity.

Man is the greatest enemy of the coyote, and the coyote knows it. So the more involvement it has with humans, the more cautious it must become to survive. In fact, I have been in some areas where all the animals, not just coyotes, appeared to be paranoid. This clearly demonstrates that animals have more brains than we often give them credit for.

Some coyotes are smarter than others, but that is part of the challenge of predator hunting.

OF DIPLOMATS AND DUNCES

Various factors play a role in the level of intelligence a creature possesses. Genetics is certainly one of these. Some kinds of information are inherent, already present at birth.

Experience is another key factor. Just like humans, animals remember when and where something good or bad happened to them. Through training as youngsters and by trial and error, they learn what to seek out and what to avoid. When prey animals make a mistake, it's often their last, but for the hunter, it's an opportunity to improve the method of hunting. The lessons we learn aid us in creating a hunting philosophy.

ROLE REVERSAL

The philosophy of any hunter should begin with reversing the roles of hunter and hunted. Think about how you would react if

Good hunters learn from their mistakes; each encounter is a chance to improve hunting skills.

you knew you might possibly be living the final moments of your life. Would you avoid such a life-threatening circumstance if you could? Of course. Humans, well, most humans anyway, strive to avoid such situations. This is why our society has so many kinds of warning devices.

Animals, however, have only their own senses to warn them of the hunter's deadly presence, although we often do a good job of helping them. I touched on this in an earlier chapter, but now I'd like to take it a step further. The highest population of humans per square mile in this country is found east of the Mississippi River, and this has a profound influence on the animals we hunt.

COMPETITIVE COMRADES

Today, some eastern states not only harbor some of the highest human populations, but also the highest numbers of hunters. Some of these states can claim over a million deer hunters, many of which hunt predators, as well. This means that a lot of hunting areas receive a lot of pressure.

Hunters who go afield with different levels of experience and different attitudes can expect different outcomes to the hunt. Unfortunately, some folks do little more than pretend to be predator hunters. This gives them a legitimate reason to sit in their cars and blow callers through the window. If a mentally defective animal happens to appear, they blast away.

The true predator hunter is a different breed altogether. A true hunter of predators knows he must first *become* a predator. He knows success depends on denying his quarry any hope of escape. His senses are always in tune to the surroundings, and he never diverts his attention from the prospects of victory. Every mistake is learned from, adding to the storehouse of knowledge that can be relied on during future hunts. The mind of a predator hunter is never at rest while he practices his craft.

He constantly seeks to unravel the mysteries before him. He thrives on success, but isn't discouraged by defeat. He respects what nature has given him and never takes it for granted. He is a man of morals and is confident in his abilities to succeed as both hunter and human.

UNREALISTIC EXPECTATIONS

I'd like to talk a little about the illusion of the hunter who never fails. The hunter who can use a predator caller like the Pied Piper used his flute. I've read about such hunters in magazines on occasion, but in all my years, I've never actually hunted with one anywhere.

I can say with pride that I've hunted with some extremely fine hunters in extremely target-rich environments. I have attended hunts where two hunters compiled double-digit scores during the course of a day. But to do this on a regular basis, even in the West, is impossible. I've gone for days, hunting hard, without popping a cap on a critter. This is one of the reasons I view eastern coyotes and bobcats as such special trophies.

I feel that hunters, particularly eastern hunters, should have realistic expectations when they head afield. Set your goals according to the availability of game, your skill level, and existing conditions. Don't worry about trying to kill five or six critters a day. Concentrate on killing one at a time. This philosophy will aid you in accomplishing the most important goal of all, collecting that first kill. Then pursue the next one with exactly the same mentality. In most cases, you will end the day with more pelts to your credit and a more positive attitude for tomorrow.

PHIL THE PHILOSOPHER

Phillip and I grew up together. Only a year separated us in school, with him the elder. Phil lived in town, I lived far out in the country. The town folks usually looked on country boys as inferior beings, except during football and hunting season.

Unlike me, Phil had little to complain about when it came to getting something he wanted. He always had it a little better than the next guy. Shotguns, dogs, clothing, it didn't matter; Phil's stuff was the best, and he was more than happy to tell you about it. But even with all this help, Phil always came up short at the end of a hunt.

Phil always had an explanation for why his expensive shotgun missed a bird. Usually, the culprit seemed to be faulty ammunition. None of his custom-crafted duck callers ever seemed to sound right to a mallard's ears. The arrows he lost had always fallen from his new quiver. I often recovered these arrows in the vicinity of Phil's treestand. They always indicated a clean miss, and I was happy to accept his donations. The bottom line was that Phil tried to buy success instead of work for it.

He never realized that a predator doesn't know the difference between a $100 rifle and a $1,000 rifle. The key is to have a rifle that is accurate and will perform in your own hands. Nothing replaces skill, knowledge, and reliable equipment. These three factors, along with a positive attitude, will get you more fur than anything else I can think of.

The frame of mind we carry into the field plays a major factor in how we perform as hunters.

ULTIMATE AMBUSH AREAS

The successful hunter must always think like a predator. In most cases, this means figuring out how a given predator might search for its next meal. In the East, much of a predator's search for food will be conducted along what's called an ecotone.

An ecotone is a transition zone between one ecosystem and another. An example of an ecotone would be where the edge of a

This hunter has positioned himself where open desert country meets thicker brush. Such transitional areas, called ecotones, often attract predators and their prey.

field joins a wooded area. Predators instinctively know that by following an ecotone they are more likely to find food, as these areas offer unique combinations of food sources and cover that prey utilize. In some ways, it's like the predator is traveling in the middle of an all-you-can-eat buffet.

The key is to know what prey species exist within the given environment. This will lead you to specific ambush locations and provide you with information about what calls to use.

Don't be afraid to try new methods for creating your own ultimate ambush sites, no matter how bizarre. If nothing else, you may gain additional knowledge about your adversary.

The coyote will test a hunter like few other animals. Their sharp senses, intelligence, and natural instincts for survival make them seem invincible at times. But the hunter who works from a sound philosophy and practices his craft skillfully can conquer even the wisest of creatures.

Chapter

11

TRICKS OF THE TRADE

A quarter of an hour had passed since I had left the warmth of my partner's truck. I was settled in at the designated calling site and had the FoxPro electronic caller doing its job. If things worked as planned, the gates of the coyote hereafter would soon be opening.

Within the first few minutes of calling I spotted five coyotes rapidly approaching. Three of them appeared to be much more eager than the other two, which trailed several yards behind. I carefully drew my rifle into position while keeping an eye on the advancing pack.

A quick inspection led me to believe the last coyote in the group was the dominant male. It was the most cautious and had the largest body. He would have to be the first target.

At the crack of the gun, the large coyote dropped in its tracks. I immediately reloaded and took aim on the other trailer. This one I judged to be the dominant female. It stopped to look at its fallen mate—the last gesture it would ever make.

The remaining three coyotes had now halted their advance and stood looking around in bewilderment. It was all the opportunity I needed, and pulled the trigger again. This time, on hearing the rifle's report, the remaining two high-tailed it for safety. I snapped off two more quick shots, but they did no damage. Still, I had three coyotes on the ground because I knew the habits of the coyote and used them to my advantage.

Soon I heard the truck returning. The smile on my face informed my partner of our success. Now it would be my turn to do the driving while he tried his luck with our somewhat unorthodox hunting technique.

SWAP THE STOP

Simply traveling into a hunting area can often alert animals to our presence, which is why it's so important to minimize noise. This is not always possible, though, due to engine noise, crunchy gravel roads, and other unavoidable aspects of travel. But when

Understanding the coyote's physical characteristics and behavior will help you determine which animals in a pack should be targeted first to take full advantage of the opportunity. (FWS)

two or more hunters work as a team, such noises can actually improve the hunting. In fact, in certain situations, predators may learn to like the sound of a vehicle.

Predators often find their meals along roadways, as vehicles run over a wide variety of prey. Also, as sad as it is, roadways are where many unwanted pets are abandoned. So these corridors often become prime hunting areas. This is where the swap-the-stop technique can really pay off.

This technique involves nothing more than having a driver let the hunter, or hunters, out of the vehicle before driving away. The key is to avoid betraying your presence by slamming the vehicle door or getting out in a wide-open area.

Experience has also led me to believe that it's better to keep the motor running while departing the vehicle. This helps cover any noise the hunters make. Starting and stopping the engine may alarm the animals.

BAITING

Coyotes and foxes love to eat carrion. So in rural areas, bait sites can be established to lure these animals. The key is to establish these sites so the hunter has the advantage and not the predator.

The first step is to gain the landowner's permission. Some folks don't like to have carrion placed on their property. But there are farmers and ranchers who despise coyotes and foxes so much that they will do anything to combat them.

The next step is to figure out the proper location for the bait. This is important, as you can't just plop bait down anywhere and expect to do well. The location should be one where the animal will be exposed in the open over the bait but that has a good stand site with cover. I usually prefer sites where there's no cover around the bait for at least one hundred yards, which allows me to get off multiple shots if needed.

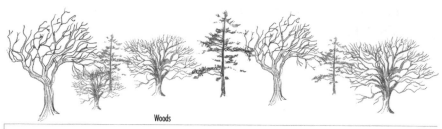

Woods

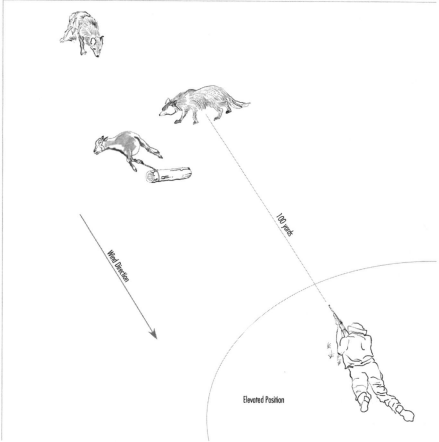

Wind Direction

100 yards

Elevated Position

Hunting Over Bait

The bait can be almost any kind of carrion. In fact, farmers and ranchers often dump lost livestock in specific locations. These are among my favorite places, as the animals are already familiar with them. The remains of a big game kill can also be used as bait. But you'll need to anchor the stuff to prevent predators from dragging it off.

The ambush site should be located downwind of the bait. Generally, I try to keep the range around 100 to 150 yards. Clear away any brush that could obstruct your view of the target zone, but don't overdo it. You'll still need to be able to approach and enter the ambush site without ever seeing the bait. If you can see the bait on your way in, critters taking it could spot you.

Ambush sites should be located on elevated ground when possible. This not only provides the hunter with a better, safer position for shooting, but also allows for an easier approach. When high ground isn't available, set up near ditches, dry streambeds, or along other types of cover that allow you to slip into position undetected.

Make sure the ambush site is ready to hunt from, too. Have a solid shooting rest available and leave something there you can sit or lie down on. You may spend hours in this spot, so you'd better be comfortable. And comfortable hunters move around less.

Prime times for hunting bait sites are the last two hours of daylight, as predators are usually just leaving their dens at this time. In extremely cold temperatures, I've also found the midday hours productive.

BIG, BAD, AND DEAD

Three days of hard hunting had passed, and I had little to show for my efforts. There was plenty of coyote sign in the area, along with all kinds of human sign. There was no doubt that the critters had been pounded pretty hard and were extremely call-shy. Now

I had to decide whether to pack up and travel somewhere else or try something different.

The following morning dawned cold and clear. The sounds of several vehicles creeping along the gravel road informed me I was not alone. Frustration filled my thoughts as I played a chorus on my E-Z Howler caller. But within seconds of repeating the call I heard a response from a lone coyote echo through the trees. I quickly grabbed my vest and rifle and started walking toward the sound. Frustration turned to hope as I scanned the terrain for a likely calling site.

I finally located a large oak tree on top of a small ridge that looked like it might work. I carefully raked the ground with my foot, and placed my FoxPro approximately twenty yards in front of the stand site. I was just about to hit the button on the remote when a thought occurred to me. Maybe I should use a different calling sound than I had before. Instead of using a single calling sound, I decided to duplicate the sounds of a lesser predator capturing prey. I hoped this might be enough to lure in a call-shy coyote.

The sounds of a distressed kitten echoed for approximately a minute. Then, with the push of a button, the sounds of fighting foxes filled the air. As quickly as I had started the caller, I stopped it. Silence dominated the woods as I scanned the ground before me. I checked around for another minute before pushing a button to simulate a single fox in distress.

Just as the call started, I detected movement among the trees. Instantly, I knew it was sunlight reflecting from the fur of a coyote. To my surprise, I soon detected another coyote several yards to the right of the first one.

Trembling with anticipation now, I centered the first coyote in the scope. I released the rifle's safety and unleashed the .22/250. The coyote instantly dropped onto the carpet of leaves. I reloaded in a flash as the second coyote slid to a stop. It appeared to be confused by the noise and the disappearance of its companion, which was its final mistake.

In the excitement, I leapt to my feet. Just then I saw another coyote hightailing it through the trees. I felt like a fool, having committed a bad mistake, but it passed quickly as I walked over to inspect the two downed coyotes.

Since that day I don't hesitate to use distressed sounds in conjunction with other noises. Giving the impression that a lesser predator has scored will often bring larger predators running. This method of calling should only be used in areas where the animals have become call-shy, though. It's a great technique, but eventually the animals will become educated.

OL' DUDE

Using dogs to hunt coyotes is nothing new. In most instances, hunters use a dog to detect a responding coyote. Dogs may also be used to lure the coyote into range by chasing and teasing it. My friend's dog, Dude, would do all this and then some. He could call coyotes in with the most agonizing, pleading howl I've ever heard. My friend had only to tie Dude to a bush or tree and the dog would cry a river of tears. Scores of coyotes were sent to that great gut pile in the sky as a result.

Dude was without question the ugliest darn dog I've ever seen. He stood about twenty-four inches high and weighed around that same number. His reddish, blackish, grayish hair reminded me of a worn-out scrubbing pad. His short ears flopped against his head whenever he moved, and he smelled like a gut-shot coyote.

But he was no dummy. He knew the second his master slipped the rope around his neck that it was show time. Maybe it was just the thought of being tied up that made him sing that

A well-trained dog can greatly increase the hunter's odds for success.

agonizing song. Perhaps it was the sound of a gun being loaded. I never did find out, but he would begin screaming and howling with the closing of the rifle's bolt.

Ol' Dude would usually spot a responding coyote long before we did. This got him so excited that he often lay down and started whining like a lost puppy. The coyotes simply couldn't resist this and would rush right to their dooms. After the shooting stopped, Dude would spring to his feet and happily bark at the dead coyotes. It was quite a performance, and I've never seen another dog that could match him.

Hunters will find that having a well-trained coyote dog is a real bonus. Not only do dogs aid in detecting and luring coyotes, but they also help recover cripples. So if you're looking for partner that won't make fun of your shooting, try hunting with a dog.

RUN AND GUN

Land Between the Lakes (LBL) is a national recreation area shared by the states of Kentucky and Tennessee. It's bordered on the east by Lake Barkley and on the west by Kentucky Lake. LBL is a sportsman's paradise, and generally hosts a very good coyote population. This also draws countless hunters prospecting for fur. If you enjoy hunting pressured predators, LBL is the place to be.

A few years back, a friend and I decided to camp in the wilds of LBL for a few days. Our main purpose was to try our luck at collecting some bobcat and coyote fur, but it turned out to be quite a learning experience.

The education began in the pre-dawn darkness of the first morning. As soon as the E-Z Howler's call ripped through the darkness, the air filled with responses from every direction. Dozens of coyotes yelped and howled while my companion bounced with excitement beside me. I didn't share his enthusiasm, though, because I immediately noticed there were no single or double responses coming, only the cries of numerous coyotes bunched together.

Soon the sun was up and we were still hunting hard. Two forty-minute stands had been completed with nothing to show for

A howling device is great for locating coyotes in an area, and it will often lure them in, as well.

our efforts. This puzzled us, as we knew we were in the vicinity of where we had first heard the coyotes.

We spent the remainder of the morning sneaking into the areas where we had heard coyotes and then calling. Nothing. Not a single hair or the sound of an alarm bark. Frustrated, we returned to camp to rest and prepare for the evening hunt.

Like the morning hunt, our evening outing was fruitless. Bewildered by our first day, we sat in our tent that night and listened to scores of coyotes yelping and howling in every direction. In fact, the darn things kept us awake most of the night. My sleep was also troubled by thoughts of the countless fresh piles of scat I had noted while we moved about. Many of the scat piles showed the remains of deer, which I found somewhat odd, as deer season had expired many weeks prior to our hunt.

The next morning, we quietly prepared breakfast by the light of a lantern. Sounds of coyotes continued to echo through the tent walls while we ate. My frustration mounted as I marked the locations of the screaming coyotes on the map. Dawn was still an hour away as we drove in to make contact with our potential victims.

We decided to set up on the last pack we had heard, and then work our way back through the designated locations. This run-and-gun technique would increase our odds, if the critters cooperated.

The first stand began with me playing a series of calls with the Knight & Hale Ultimate 1. This caller has lured many a call-shy predator to its demise, but even this was not doing the trick. Dawn's faint colors painted the horizon while we continued to hope and wait. Suddenly, I heard a pack of coyotes begin to yelp in the distance. This continued for a couple of minutes or so before I detected another sound, which I instantly recognized as a deer in distress. As quickly as the sounds had begun, they ceased.

I looked over at my partner to see if he too had heard the sounds. He had, and we both knew it was time for a change. I now suspected why the coyotes were traveling in groups. Evidently, they were hunting in packs to increase their odds of capturing larger prey. In this area, larger prey meant deer, abandoned dogs, or anything else that crossed their paths.

Soon we had arrived in our next designated location and were preparing the calling site. This entailed placing two electronic callers, one of which I would set to play canine distress sounds. My friend operated the second caller, playing the sounds of fighting coyotes. We hoped this would create the illusion that a coyote had found a dinner of dog meat and needed help.

The callers had been playing for approximately ten minutes when I saw my companion lift his shotgun and fire, following up with two more shots. It was my turn next, as a single coyote darted in front of me. I unleashed my shotgun and watched the coyote roll over.

Several minutes passed while we waited to see if any more coyotes had a death wish. After a quarter of an hour, we silenced the callers. With three coyotes in tow, we headed back to the truck. Our experiment had paid off, as it has countless other times since then. Now we have a proven calling technique for coping with a change in the coyote's habits. The key to our success was in closely observing the prevailing conditions and making the necessary adjustments.

OLD SATAN

There will be times when a serious predator hunter will encounter a coyote he learns to purely hate. In most instances, it will be an animal with some sort of unusual markings or characteristics. You will eventually be able to identify the animal the instant you see or hear it. Satan was just that kind of coyote.

My first dealings with Satan came on a very cold and cloudy morning a few years ago. I was hunting solo on some private land where I really wanted to make a good showing for the owner. He had had some young sheep killed, along with one of his prized beagles. The owner despised coyotes like few people I've ever known, which really made me want to do well for him.

The first day of hunting yielded only a single coyote and a bobcat. I figured this would make the owner happy, but when I met him that afternoon he was visibly upset. Two more lambs were missing from the east pasture.

The pasture consisted of several hundred acres, with a long ridge of hardwood forest bordering its northern end. Most of the sheep had been killed on the northern end, so it was pretty obvious where the culprits were coming from. This would be my primary area of operation the next morning.

Dawn was still thirty minutes away when I planted my rump on the frozen ground. A large oak tree located in the pasture would serve as my backrest and block my outline. I felt good about this location and readied the electronic caller and rifle.

Light was showing on the horizon when I touched the switch of the caller. The sounds of a Johnny Stewart Super Jack tape began blaring across the timbered ridge. Anticipation kept me warm while I scanned the area for an approaching coyote. Then I heard a sound from the ridge. I quickly reduced the caller's volume to identify what I was hearing. I soon recognized the warning barks of a coyote. Anger filled me, as this bark would put any other coyotes in the area on alert about my presence.

I began scanning the hillside with binoculars. In a matter of seconds, I spotted the coyote returning my stare from its perch on a large rock. It appeared much darker than most coyotes I had seen, and its manner betrayed no fear as it sat proudly on its throne.

The odds were against my getting a bullet that far, so there wasn't much to do but gather up my belongings. The damned coyote continued its barking as I walked back to the truck. In fact, to my burning ears, the frequency had increased to the point that it now sounded a lot like a laugh.

I continued to hunt the ranch for the rest of the morning and managed to hammer another coyote. But the more I thought about what had happened that morning, the angrier I became.

I didn't have a chance to return to the east pasture for several days. When I arrived, I headed for the same location before dawn. Nearly an hour passed before I could see shapes through the riflescope. When I felt it was safe I pushed the switch of the caller and the sounds of a distressed puppy filled the air.

I scanned the area for several minutes as the caller played on, stopping occasionally to grin at the toy dog sitting beside the speaker. I felt very confident as golden streaks of sunlight crawled across the frosty pasture. Suddenly I detected movement at the edge of the woods and knew it was a coyote. The sunlight reflecting from its fur made it shine like a new penny. Then another coyote appeared only yards to the left of the first one. I slowly began shouldering the rifle.

The coyotes had stepped into the pasture and were trotting toward me. I could already taste the thrill of victory as I peered over the riflescope to watch them. But then both animals slammed on the brakes. I snapped to full attention as a coyote's bark sounded from the ridge. Instantly, I knew it was the same coyote that had fouled my plans on the previous hunt. I could only watch helplessly as the other two coyotes bolted for the cover of the woods.

Angrily, I leapt from my position and hurled a few curses at the barking demon. Frustration melted whatever chill I might have felt as I gathered my equipment and listened to the coyote continue its laughter. Now it would be nothing short of an all-out war.

Later that day I saw the landowner and told him what had happened. Like me, he was pretty ticked off about missing the chance of nailing two sheep-eating coyotes. I asked his permission to allow a friend to accompany me on the next hunt and he readily agreed.

The following afternoon I scouted the ridge where old Satan was making me miserable. I noted several scat piles around the big rock. I also took note of the view the old devil had of the entire pasture. It was a nice setup, and I couldn't help but admire the coyote for a few seconds before continuing my inspection. Almost on top of the ridge, I found a fallen tree that afforded an

When a tough coyote forces you to change your plans, use whatever cover the terrain provides.

excellent view of old Satan's throne from a distance of approximately one hundred yards.

For almost a week, high winds prevented me from unveiling my plan. But finally things changed. Only a slight breeze drifted down the ridge as I slowly maneuvered in the darkness. It was still an hour before the sky would signal the start of another day.

I listened to the howling of a distant coyote as I settled in, automatically making a mental note of its location. Only a thin, pale line of light marked the horizon when I heard my companion driving the gravel road beside the field. Then the headlights became visible at the far end of the pasture.

After another fifteen minutes I could vaguely make out my partner coming toward me across the pasture. Everything was right on schedule, and it was hard to suppress my excitement.

Soon the sounds of a fox in distress began echoing from my friend's caller down in the pasture. I scanned the surrounding woods for movement. Nothing. After several minutes of listening, I could feel disappointment seeping into my thoughts. Little voices in my mind began telling me the crafty old coyote had again beaten me at my own game. Suddenly the report of a rifle roared from the pasture, then another.

I scanned my partner's position in the pasture with binoculars, but as there were well over seven hundred yards between us, I could see nothing of interest. Still, I continued searching the pasture for a glimpse of a corpse. With my concentration so focused, I was completely startled by the loud, mournful howl that erupted near my position.

I dropped the binoculars and found myself staring full view at Satan sitting on the rock. Surprise left me paralyzed for a few moments as I watched the coyote raise its head and scream into the sky. Then my instincts took over, and I was peering through the riflescope with the crosshairs centered on the animal's shoulder. I tripped the trigger of the .280 Remington rifle, sending the 120-grain bullet right where I wanted it to go. I had no intention of allowing the coyote any mercy.

The recoil left my eyes above the scope, and I watched as the coyote spun through the air. Like a rag doll being hit by a speeding semi, it flipped several times before landing in the leaves. He was dead, damn good and dead. He'd been smart, but his habits had betrayed him.

I dragged the remains of old Satan from the ridge and joined my partner in the pasture, where he told me he'd accounted for two more. Maybe the devilish coyote sensed it was his day to die and just wanted some company.

Chapter
12

WEATHER OR NOT

The rain pelting the tent canvas woke us from a very restful sleep. The weatherman had been right, for a change. If he continued his lucky streak, the rain would cease in a few hours and turn to snow with the approaching cold front. My companions slowly roused from their slumber and began preparing breakfast.

Despite the steady rhythm pounding the tent roof, they suited up in rain gear and departed. I, on the other hand, crawled back into my sleeping bag to enjoy a little more of the easy life. This old dog had played that game too many times. I figured the other old dogs (coyotes) were doing the same thing. The hunting would be better in a few hours, and soaking up cold rainwater was not my idea of fun.

Within two hours, my thoroughly drenched companions returned. Their misery was expressed very clearly as they peeled wet clothes from very cold bodies. My helpful comments about human intelligence and having faith in modern weather forecasting were not appreciated. So I returned to my dreams while my buddies huddled around the heater.

I was still lying in my bedroll reading when the sounds of rain began to fade. I quickly sprang up to peek outside. Large fluffy flakes of snow were drifting down from the dark clouds above. I was as excited as a kid seeing snow for the first time. I knew the critters would stand out like torches on a dark night.

I wasted no time getting prepared while my companions dozed. I probably should have awakened them, but someone had to hunt solo, so why not me. Besides, they had already been out that day and I hadn't.

The snow was already an inch deep by the time I arrived at my first calling location, a large weed-covered field bordered by a beaver swamp. It seemed like an excellent location for luring a bobcat out of the thick undergrowth. Within minutes of playing my opening chorus of the jackrabbit blues I heard the squawking of blue jays from the swamp. This was a good indication that a predator was on its way, so I readied my shotgun and pointed the muzzle toward the birds.

I switched the caller to a close-range coaxer. Only the faint whining sounds disturbed the silence. Small birds fluttered from the weeds, informing me of the intruder's continued advance.

Smart hunters use the weather to their advantage.

Then the dark silhouette of a bobcat appeared, which I probably would not have detected without the aid of the snow.

Slowly, the bobcat continued forward inside the thick weeds. But the nice male's false sense of security soon brought him within easy range of the magnum. All I had to do was decide whether I wanted to fill my daily bag limit now or wait. I didn't think long, though. Soon the bobcat's pelt would belong to the local fur dealer, and I'd move on to other stand sites.

Darkness had fallen over our camp by the time I returned. Inside the tent, I discovered that my companions had made three stands after I left. Their single coyote and red fox, added to my bobcat and two coyotes, made a splendid showing for an afternoon of hunting. And we owed it all to the fresh snow.

WHY SNOW

Snow can affect animal behavior in many ways. Deep snows can send them into sheltered areas for days at a time, while snow levels of a few inches to a foot often expose their cover and restrict the feeding

Snow cover makes it easier to detect a responding animal.

activity of many prey species. Predators are forced to hunt harder to find prey, so they are more visible and vulnerable to hunters.

Snow also makes excellent tracking media. The knowledgeable hunter will be able to decipher the type of species and the direction of travel by examining the tracks predators can't avoid leaving. In many instances, the first hours after a fresh snow permit the hunter to track the animal quickly and ambush it.

WHINING IN THE WIND

Coyote sign was everywhere. Piles of scat dotted the roadside like spots on a leopard, and both coyote and bobcat tracks covered the ground, making it appear that we'd surely found the Promised Land. Yet our enthusiasm for the hunt was dead and gone—this was the third day in a row that the wind had blown hard.

The weatherman had predicted wind speeds of ten to fifteen miles per hour from a northerly direction. But actual conditions included wind pushing twenty-five mph, with gusts well above that. The howling sound the wind made against the truck was eerie, and the bending roadside trees served to remind us of our foolishness in being out. Disgusted, we continued driving the gravel roads and searching for sign. Hopefully, the weatherman would end up being half right and the cold front would pass during the night.

The alarm sounded loudly at three AM, and I sprang from the warmth of the blankets and ran to the door to check on the wind. Only a mild, very cold breeze greeted me. Perfect.

We gobbled down a few sweet rolls while gathering our gear. In record time, we dressed, filled the thermos jugs, and were driving off under the stars. Only a quick trip back to get my partner's coat slowed us down on the hour-long drive to our hunting grounds.

A cold but gentle breeze nipped at our noses as we stopped to try out our E-Z Howlers. Dozens of coyotes responded in the moonlight. Dawn was showing on the horizon when we finally arrived at the first of our designated locations. I removed the shotgun from the truck's gun rack and gathered a box of shells. The shotgun was my preferred choice because we would be hunting a brushy area bordering a creek bottom.

This was an excellent location, as the lower elevation of the creek bottom would serve as a protective area during high winds. We settled in and began calling. Screaming and pleading sounds emanated from the Knight & Hale Ultimate 1 for around sixty seconds or so, then silence prevailed for another two minutes before we repeated the calling sequence.

After the third sequence, I heard a faint lip squeaking from my partner. He had spied a predator and was trying to coax it closer. The tension mounted as I listened and scanned the dimly lit surroundings for a clue to the animal's whereabouts. But then a shot from his rifle shattered the silence. I could hear him reloading, and then he gave a soft whistle, which was the signal to begin calling again. We were already up one.

Before the next sequence ended, the report of his rifle again broke the silence. This time, the gun barked three times in succession, and then again a few seconds later. As I couldn't see what he was shooting at, this pattern puzzled me, but you never know what will happen when hunting predators.

I heard the rustling of dried leaves as he rose from his stand, and I quickly joined him, my curiosity overwhelming. From his expression, I could tell he had scored well. His first shot had taken a large bobcat, and the second barrage dropped two coyotes. The final shot had been a vain attempt at yet another fleeing coyote.

We gathered the trophies and quickly headed for the truck. Our confidence was up, and we both had a good feeling about our next destination; with good reason, as it turned out. We collected four more coyotes and another bobcat that morning. Such results aren't uncommon after several days of high wind, though.

WINNING IN THE WIND

Wind, especially the hard, gusting kind, probably affects animal behavior more than any other element of weather. It disrupts a predator's olfactory capabilities, even their hearing and eyesight. Wind not only distorts scent and sound, but it also creates movement throughout the habitat.

It has to be much more difficult for a predator to detect a mouse moving in a bunch of twisting and twirling weeds. There isn't much hard data to support this, but I do know that hunting is usually pretty sorry in windy conditions, which is why I prefer to wait until the wind dies down. But this isn't always possible for hunters who have only a limited amount of time afield. So if you have to hunt during windy conditions, as I sometimes have, here is my advice.

Hunt areas that provide some form of shelter for animals; areas of lower elevation that contain thick cover are best. Basins,

In windy conditions, animals often take refuge in low-lying areas.

gullies, dry riverbeds—anything that will allow the animals to get beneath the wind currents.

Call with volume, but very sparingly, in windy conditions. Wind distorts sound and weakens volume. Responding animals will often be able to locate the general area of the sound's source, but may have difficultly pinpointing it. I like to use a remote-controlled electronic caller at these times because it allows me greater flexibility in dealing with a responding animal.

Be patient, particularly if smaller predators like fox and bobcat are the primary targets. These animals not only use movement to find their own prey, but also avoid becoming prey

Be patient and stay well hidden, as wind can make already wary predators almost paranoid.

themselves by detecting their enemy's movements. These predators will appear almost paranoid when responding to the call on windy days. So be ready, as they probably won't give you a second chance.

During prolonged periods of high winds, I generally concentrate on hunting bait sites. These areas are established feeding areas, and the animals know the meal is a sure thing. I always try to keep several bait sites active so I'll have a backup or two for tough hunting conditions.

VARYING TEMPERATURES

Accurate weather forecasting has helped the hunter in many ways. Animals, like humans, are warm-blooded creatures, and extreme heat or cold can be fatal.

In most predator-hunting situations, extreme cold has the most influence over the hunt. Hunters should focus on the most likely comfort zone of a specific time period—generally the warmest phase. A good example of this might be the day or so prior to the arrival of a major cold front or several days afterward.

I have learned that animals really detest being out during the worst days of a cold front. But when prolonged periods of cold exist, the animals still must eat to survive. Hunters who are equipped to safely cope with extreme elements may discover some excellent hunting. Just remember to use common sense; hunting is supposed to be fun, not torture.

Chapter

13

HUNTING ANYTIME

The sun had baked the ground all day long and was now dropping to the western horizon. I stopped to marvel at the fiery beauty of the sunset, but the impatient grunt from my companion snapped me back to reality. I had to hurry to get the spotlight connections fitted in place so we could go hunting.

Soon we were traveling along the two ribbons of dirt my friend optimistically called a road. Stars were beginning to appear in the inky sky, and the day's heat was turning to cool night. The desert was coming alive with creatures that had taken refuge from the intense sun. Long-eared jackrabbits bounced across the roadway in front of the headlights, and a great horned owl suddenly appeared only inches from the windshield, barely escaping a collision.

Soon we spotted the glow from a reflective stickpin attached to a small block of wood. This was a marker we had previously placed to help us find the designated calling location in the dark. Things look a lot differently at night than they do in daylight, and scouting and marking calling sites can save time and head off trouble.

We stood in the bed of the pickup, quickly and quietly connecting the spotlights and loading our rifles. I started a distressed-bunny calling sequence, letting the painful cries continue for a minute or so before stopping to listen.

Thousands of stars twinkled overhead in the moonless sky, and the howl of a lone coyote echoed in the distance. After several minutes of silence, I lifted the light above my head and flipped the switch. The soft glow from the red lens cover cut through the darkness. I slowly swept the light around in a full circle, but only the shapes of prickly pear and Spanish daggers appeared.

I turned off the light and began calling again in darkness. This series lasted almost as long as the first, and again the spotlight swept over the area. But this time I used the close-range coaxer in conjunction with the light. The beam had only traveled a few feet when the glowing eyes of a coyote appeared. Like two shiny gold coins, the eyes bounced up and down through the prickly pear. The coyote was coming in fast.

With the light slightly above the approaching target, we watched while the glowing eyes grew larger. Only an occasional whimper from the coaxer disturbed the silence. When I heard the sound of my companion's safety being released I brought the light directly onto those eyes.

The coyote instantly halted its charge, which proved to be fatal. Like a boulder falling from the sky, the predator crashed to the ground. This would be the first of four coyotes to drop before the end of the night.

Today, many states permit year-round predator hunting to combat predation within their borders. Some states even permit nighttime hunting and/or offer no bag limits. Hunters should always check the regulations before hunting at night, but where it's allowed it can be deadly on predators.

I love to hunt predators anytime and anywhere, but hunting in the dark is my favorite time of all. Predators are basically nocturnal creatures, so the odds for success automatically increase when the sun goes down. And there's a special excitement in seeing a pair of glowing eyes charging you that just isn't there in the easy comfort of full light.

Your vision is restricted to just what the spotlight reveals. Then in the blink of an eye two glowing dots appear in the wilderness. Two eyes that are attached to something that thinks it wants to eat you. Carefully you prepare for the moment of truth as the eyes grow bigger. Then you whisper the command to lower the full strength of the light onto the target. It's a feeling only the predator hunter knows.

NIGHTTIME EQUIPMENT

The basic difference in daytime and nighttime equipment is the spotlight. Having used an assortment of spotlights over the years, I've developed a few preferences. First, spend the money to get a good one. Having your spotlight fail you in the middle of the night in the middle of nowhere isn't fun. Second, always carry spare bulbs. Third, use a colored lens cover, as bright light can quickly scare off game. The color of the lens cover is a more personal choice; some hunters like red over blue or amber over everything else. I like red because I seem to have fewer problems with it. The key is to keep the beam slightly above the target until it's time to shoot.

For rifle shooters, night hunting also requires good optics. The type of rifle you use can make or break the hunt. Scopes should be of good quality and have excellent light-seeking capabilities. Some scopes also feature a lighted reticle for enhanced vision. In most cases, this isn't necessary if the spotlight does its job. The same goes for night-vision gear. On the other hand, if it gives you additional confidence, it can't hurt.

Hunting at night puts you in the field when many predators are most active.

Powerful spotlights are very useful for nighttime hunting, but remember to add a colored lens cap to avoid spooking the animals you're calling in. (Cabela's)

BY THE SILVERY MOON

State regulations where I planned to hunt prohibited the use of artificial light for hunting but said nothing about restricting night hunting. I called the local conservation officer to confirm that I could legally hunt predators in the moonlight. The answer was yes, and I was as happy as a puppy with a new house slipper.

The light the full moon cast on the freshly fallen snow made it seem almost like daylight. I walked quietly to the first calling location; everything was peaceful in this winter wonderland. My excitement was more than a match for the chill of the night as I dropped down and leaned back against the big oak. Once the shotgun was loaded, I began working the manual caller. The medium-range sounds of a cottontail rabbit in distress broke over the calm countryside.

I continued repeating my calling sequence: one minute of pleading, three minutes of silence. As with daytime hunting, I would call for about thirty minutes before moving on. However, this stand proved to be a winner, and within the first ten minutes I detected movement.

The silhouettes of the coyotes against the snow instantly caught my attention. Like kamikaze pilots, the four predators came charging across the pasture toward me. I nervously raised the big magnum and directed its muzzle at the middle of the pack. Tension mounted while I waited for the chosen coyote to cut the distance to twenty yards or so. I fired as he hit the imaginary mark, and the critter slid nose-first into the snow.

The remaining coyotes immediately scattered in different directions, but their speed was no match for my magnum. The next victim tumbled in the snow, leaped up, and dropped again after another dose of lead. I sent the remaining ammunition toward the rump of another escaping villain.

I worked through three more calling sites before my next moonlight encounter. Here, a bobcat challenged the power of the magnum at extremely close range.

Hunting at night, even just by the light of the moon, is an experience you won't soon forget.

OFF-SEASON REASONS

As I alluded to above, predator hunting seasons and regulations vary from state to state. In areas where year-round hunting is allowed, spring and summer can be fun, productive times to head afield. Hunting at these times may also help local game populations, as you'll be culling predators that might wreak havoc during the nesting seasons of various gamebirds and animals. This is one of the reasons I'm always prepared for coyotes during the spring turkey season. Some hunters frown on hunting at this time

Off-season hunting is an excellent way to practice your marksmanship and keep your predator skills sharp.

Decoys are particularly effective in the spring, when coyotes are looking for nests to raid.

of year due to the possibility of shooting a pregnant female. So let your conscience be your guide. I say the more the merrier—there sure as hell isn't any lack of coyotes.

One of my favorite techniques for hunting off-season coyotes incorporates a hen turkey decoy in a nesting position. I then use the calls of a lost turkey to lure the culprits into gun range. If the timing is right, both male and female coyotes may try for a turkey dinner. If the female is already denned up with offspring, dad will be the target. Again, not everyone finds this ethical, but I think of it as a form of conservation for other game species hunters like to pursue.

The use of a fawn deer decoy in conjunction with a fawn distress caller can also be lethal on coyotes and bobcats. Anyone who thinks these predators don't eat venison should stay in front of their televisions. I have viewed some pretty gruesome scenes where predators found young game animals.

FUN IN THE SUN

The telephone rang just after I finished eating dinner. It was a local farmer informing me he had seen several coyotes hanging around the field where he'd been cutting hay. I knew this was a family group consisting of parents and young of the year. I also knew that the farmer hated coyotes, and this would be a splendid opportunity to strengthen our relationship.

After consulting with him about livestock locations, workers, houses, and other safety concerns, I committed myself for a hunt the following afternoon. With a little luck, the coyotes would return to the freshly harvested field as the heat of the day dissipated.

The midafternoon sun was beginning to drop in the western sky when I arrived. The farmer quickly pointed out where he had seen the coyotes near some adjoining woods. The coyotes took shelter there and came to the pasture to feast on the spoils of the cutting. I also noticed an abundance of grasshoppers in the field, which was like putting candy in front of a kid. Insects, rodents, and vegetation all rank high in the coyote's summertime diet.

I tested the wind and selected an ambush spot across the field from where the farmer had seen activity. In a short time, I had cleared the brush, unfolded my tarp, and prepared the rifle. The latter consisted of setting up the Harris Bipod, laying out extra ammo and binoculars, and using my Bushnell rangefinder to mark the distance to the woods. With everything ready, I retrieved a cold drink from my little cooler and sat back to await the coyotes.

Hours passed, and the sun was getting low in the sky. Darkness was less than an hour away, and I was becoming a little concerned. Then I noticed something odd just inside the woods from where I thought the coyotes would come. I slowly retrieved the binoculars and peered at the object, a coyote. It stood still, staring in my direction. Had it spotted me?

I waited for the coyote to make its move. Would it turn back into the woods? Enter the pasture? Was there another standing behind it? Should I attempt a shot and gamble on just one coyote? It was hard to be patient, as the anticipation was making me nervous.

I began creeping the rifle into position. One coyote was better than nothing, so I focused the crosshairs on the target. Suddenly it turned and looked over its shoulder. I knew this was a good indication that others were behind it. Soon, another adult critter and four smaller ones joined the coyote. Happily, the youngsters bounced into the pasture and began chasing grasshoppers. The first adult followed while the other sat down on its haunches. The last one would be my primary target.

The coyote collapsed instantly at the crack of the rifle. I quickly worked the rifle bolt to reload, as the others were frozen by their confusion. This allowed me enough time to focus on the second adult and drop it in its tracks. In less than a minute, the entire group had been eliminated. I knew the farmer would be happy, and that I'd have some new fall hunting grounds—all thanks to an off-season predator hunt.

ONE MORE THING

While hunting predators during nontraditional time periods can keep us sharp and strengthen hunter/landowner relationships, it may also educate the predators to the ways of man. Off-season calling usually takes place in extremely warm temperatures, which make it that much easier for animals to detect the hunter's scent. Also, the sounds of a distressed animal may not be as appealing due to the abundance of other food sources.

I like off-season hunting, but it should only be done on a limited basis when the hunter feels it's justified.

Chapter
14

HUNTING PUBLIC LAND

Fifteen or twenty minutes had passed since I used my E-Z Howler caller to mimic a lone female in love and received a very distant response. Now my long-time hunting partner, David, and I lay waiting in ambush.

Nestled on the other side of the big tree, I could hear David slowly chewing his beloved Juicy Fruit. The rhythm of his actions was as distinctive as it was annoying. But knowing a coyote was on its way made life more bearable, and I tried to block everything else from my mind.

Time continued to slowly tick away. Boredom is often a factor when howling for coyotes, particularly when the responding animal has to travel a good distance. And as I hadn't shot anything in days, I was impatient for something to happen. It's easy to start questioning whether or not you should call again, even while knowing full well you shouldn't. This was the mental debate I was having when David suddenly whispered, "You're not going to believe this."

Normally, I would have heard the release of his rifle's safety or the eruption of his .22/250. Never had I heard him talk while waiting for a coyote. So I immediately responded, "What?"

With a hint of disgust, he indicated that I should peek around the tree. Another hunter was slowly creeping toward us. The gentleman was camouflaged from head to toe and was carrying a scoped rifle. I told David to lay still and keep quiet. He did, and within minutes the man had stalked to within a few yards of us.

I said "How ya doin'?" in a normal tone of voice, but the poor guy still jumped out of his skin. It took him a few moments for him to collect himself, and then he asked what in the hell we were doing there.

I asked him the same question. He said he was coyote hunting and had heard a coyote howling in our immediate area. He also informed us, in a rather snotty way, that if we hadn't intruded on his hunt he might have gotten the coyote. Just then, I heard David's chewing gum pop, and our new friend again got quite a fright.

Hunting public land means dealing with other hunters and pressured animals, but if you do your homework you'll still find plenty of game.

PLANNING

When venturing onto public hunting ground, always remember that these lands have probably already received a lot of pressure (unless it's the first day of the hunting season). The next thing to take into consideration is your ability to cope with things that could annoy or anger you. Never forget you are in the land of the yahoo—hunters who often know a little but think they know a lot. Yahoos generally don't mess up intentionally, but are simply too ignorant or unskilled to know what they've done. If you hunt much, I'm sure you've met a few of these folks.

Hunters heading to public lands with expectations for taking high predator numbers will usually be disappointed. I look at anything I collect from public hunting land as a bonus for the season. I'm not saying public land is a bust, of course, but it can offer some of the most difficult hunting you'll ever find. On the other hand, it can provide some really fine hunting at times.

One of my favorite public hunting lands is the Land Between the Lakes (LBL), a piece of country I alluded to earlier. The beauty and abundant game populations of this vast semiwilderness have captivated me since the late 1960s. I've hunted and camped within its boundaries literally for weeks at a time.

LBL has been my schooling ground for hunting wild turkey, whitetail, and the coyote and bobcat. And I've learned the ways of the yahoo here like nowhere else I've ever hunted. In fact, I've studied the ways of the yahoo so closely that some of my friends think I'm getting paranoid. I take this as a compliment, as it means that

Topographic maps are a huge help in identifying likely areas to hunt.

I'm constantly sharpening my skills. I'm always thinking ahead to my next move when I'm on public ground.

I like to start my planning by checking to see if any special hunting dates might coincide with my hunting time. Many public lands have their own schedule for big game and small game hunts, and often as not, the big game hunts are on a quota system. This means that a specific number of hunters will be in the woods at a specific time. Trying to lure a coyote into range when you're surrounded by hundreds of deer hunters is not exactly a smart idea.

So when possible, avoid hunting these areas on weekends or during other times of peak activity. Instead, use these periods to scout for sign and note where the weekend warriors are going. This will give you a great handle on which areas are the most pressured. I have also learned that it doesn't hurt to communicate with other hunters on occasion. Acting like a yahoo can save you a lot of time in the long run. If you can learn what type of caller they're using, you'll have a better chance of offering predators something different during your hunt.

I always like to wait until the middle of the week to hunt public areas, which gives the animals a chance to catch their breath after the weekend rush.

LEARNING FROM THE GOOD GUYS

Public grounds are always highly competitive places. To say the least, brotherly love doesn't run too high among hunters trying to achieve the same results. So it's often necessary to outsmart our brother hunters as well as the game we pursue. I learned this the hard way while competing in a predator-hunting contest on public land.

The contest was in its second day, and only one team had really done well. I knew those guys were excellent hunters. The

Clubs often sponsor predator-hunting competitions on public land.

problem was that I thought I was a good hunter too, yet had nothing to show for it. Either those hunters really had something going on or they had been extremely lucky. It was something I was determined to find out.

The mystery surrounding their success began to unravel when I noticed their truck parked on the side of the road. I instructed my partner to slow down so I could jump out without him stopping the vehicle. Then I told him to pick me up in half an hour, after I had a chance to spy on the successful hunters.

I took refuge in a stand of cedar trees while waiting for the sounds of my partner's truck to fade. My main concerns were not messing up the other hunters' stand and not getting shot. I just wanted to see, or rather listen, to what they were doing.

I waited and listened for several minutes but heard nothing but the chirping of birds. Suddenly a single rifle shot echoed in the distance, which was puzzling as I'd heard no calling at all. Fifteen minutes later I saw the hunters approaching. From my hiding place, I could see that they weren't carrying any kind of electronic caller as they flopped the single coyote into the truck. It had to be their first of the day, as I hadn't noticed anything else in the truck bed.

Just as they were driving away, my partner returned to get me. I sat tight until the other truck disappeared, then hurried out to flag down my ride. We quickly turned the truck around and trailed the other hunters from a distance. After a mile or so of driving and stopping to listen, we heard the other vehicle come to a halt. Several minutes later, we repeated the drop-off plan. But this time I dug into my daypack for a set of hearing enhancers. I was determined to find out just what they were up to.

I was shocked at the sounds I thought I heard them making, and even more shocked by how quickly the next blaze of gunfire occurred. A volley of at least six rifle shots echoed from their position.

I raced to the road and was soon picked up by my partner. He asked me if I had heard all the shooting, and the expression on my face was answer enough. He continued to drive at a normal speed until we'd put a mile or so behind us. We pulled over and had a cup of coffee while I told him what I thought I'd heard with the hearing enhancers. He was as surprised as I'd been, and even asked me to say it over again.

We both sat quietly for a moment, and then he asked yet again if I was sure about what I'd heard. But there was no question about it. Having raised two children of my own, I knew without doubt that I'd heard the sounds of a crying human baby.

I never would have guessed that a tape recording of a screaming baby would change the way I hunt, but knowing we were already licked, I elected to take advantage of the situation.

First, we had to turn around and locate our competitor's vehicle again.

We found it later that morning, and my partner slowly drove past. I received yet another surprise when I glanced into their truck bed. There was nothing there. Not a single hair, let alone the entire body of a coyote. We knew they had collected one coyote, as we had seen them cross the field with it. The cloak-and-dagger style of these hunters was really beginning to intrigue me: stashing their kills, unorthodox calling sounds, and who knows what else.

We spent the rest of the day trying to lure a coyote into range so we'd at least have something to show for ourselves. It took us until the last stand before check-in to finally collect one. Along with about half the other teams, we made our appearance with but a single dog. The good fellows added five more to their tally for a landslide victory.

Congratulations were in order, and while we chatted with the winning team they questioned us about why we kept driving around them. Sheepishly, I told them what we had done and half-heartedly apologized for my actions. This gave them a good laugh, as they informed me they had done the same thing to me the previous year.

You just never know what to expect when hunting public land, but it usually pays to be crafty.

Chapter
15

HUNTING FOXES AND RACCOONS

I slowly directed the muzzle of my shotgun toward the glowing eyes of a gray fox. The animal's fast and incautious approach had given it away. The roar of the gun shattered the night. Only the light reflected in the predator's eyes marked where it lay. Like the two before it, this fox had responded to the distressed sounds of a woodpecker.

Now I would gather my bounty and travel approximately a mile to hunt the edge of a large cornfield, where I planned to lure a red fox into shotgun range as I had done on other occasions. But if a gray appeared first, well, it would just have to join the others in the back of my truck.

THE RED FOX

Many species and subspecies of fox are found across North America: the red, gray, swift, kit, and arctic fox. The average hunter will usually encounter just two of these, the red or gray fox.

The red fox (*Vulpes fulva*) runs around ten to fifteen pounds, depending on sex and region. The red's head and body

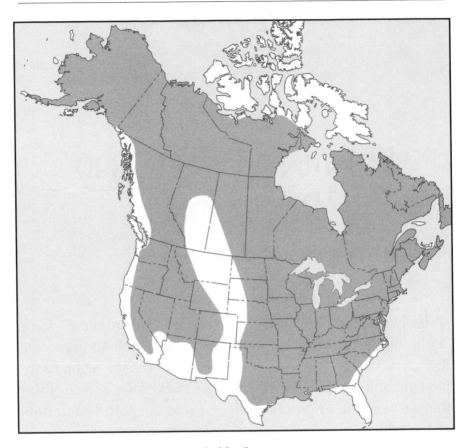

Red Fox Range

range from twenty-one to twenty-five inches, with the tail adding another thirteen to sixteen inches. The red fox resembles a small dog, and its coat is normally reddish-yellow (darkest on the back), with a white belly. The bushy tail is mixed with black hairs and tipped with white; the legs and feet are black.

Hunters may find many color variations, such as darker areas over the shoulder and down the middle of the back. The red fox also occurs in a black phase, often referred to as silver. This phase appears black overall, with white-tipped body hairs and white tips on the tail.

Coloration gives the red fox its name.

The red fox generally prefers a habitat of a mixed forest and open terrain. Fields bordered by brushy fencerows or drainage ditches are also excellent places to find them. Open areas that contain rock piles and/or dozer piles can also become preferred habitats.

Like most predators, the red fox is generally most active during periods of low light and at night. But it may resort to daytime activity to avoid encountering other predators, especially where coyotes are abundant.

Its menu consists of virtually anything from insects, fruits, and berries to large rabbits, rodents, and birds. During periods of extreme cold, the red fox may convert to feeding on carrion.

It delivers young of the year during the months of March and April, depending on latitude, after a gestation period of about fifty-one days. Litters generally include four to nine pups, with only one per household each year.

This is excellent fox habitat.

OL' SLY

The old saying "sly as a fox" has a lot of merit. During my early days of predator hunting, the red fox was my primary target whenever I tooted on a predator caller. It was the most hated animal of my rural community, being notorious for raiding hen houses or snatching up rabbits and quail. Dropping the hammer on one of these super-suspicious creatures was often difficult, but with knowledge gained from some of my elders and by honing my skills, I eventually learned to outfox "Ol' Sly."

One of the first things I learned about cashing in on reds was to never underestimate the critter. Unlike some predators, I think the red fox is paranoid before it even leaves its mother's womb, and just keeps getting jumpier as it grows. I've watched reds pace back and forth a hundred yards away from the calling stand or pace around in a circle looking suspiciously at a live rabbit or

This is as wary a predator as you'll ever find.

chicken I staked out, only to have them disappear, seemingly without provocation.

Such experiences led me to develop a firm policy pertaining to reds: Kill 'em when you can and never try to predict what they'll do. This policy helped me dramatically increase my numbers before Mr. Red changed its ways.

The change I refer to resulted from the coyote's invasion of the eastern portion of the country. The red fox suddenly had a new and deadly enemy. To survive, it now had to become even more paranoid, which required me to refine my hunting technique.

REBOUNDING REDS

My annual tally of red fox hides was growing smaller and smaller. And the number of reds I was losing on my trap line each year was increasing. My gun numbers were even worse. In fact, I completely stopped trying to call red fox for several years. It wasn't until the mid-1990s that I began to notice more red fox in my area.

The first bunch of reds I discovered were within the city limits of a neighboring town. They had converted an abandoned woodchuck den into their home. The family consisted of mom, dad, and five youngsters. I spied on the family several times during the course of the summer.

By autumn, I noticed that only the two adult foxes used the den. This was not surprising, as I knew foxes usually sent their youngsters out on their own fairly early. I decided it might be nice to call the foxes and shoot them with my camera instead of a gun. The last thing I wanted to do was hamper their chances for increasing the population.

So one morning I slipped into the area before dawn and readied my calling site and camera. I hadn't lured a red fox into close range in several years, and I was quivering with anticipation. Soon, the dawning sun sent shafts of light over the frost-covered ground, creating a beautiful scene. I directed the caller toward the den and sent a gentle low-volume series of the bunny blues across the small field.

After several minutes of silence, I unleashed another series of calls. This time I saw one of the foxes emerge from the den. A charge of excitement went through me as I watched the fox move a few yards in my direction. Then, as if someone had ignited a bomb, the fox turned and dove back inside the den. Puzzled, I checked the air currents, thinking the gentle cross breeze had shifted. But it hadn't. I quickly produced another series of calls. After nearly an hour of trying to coax the critter from its den, I gave up.

I turned the scene over in my mind all day. I had seen reds do some weird things, but never something like that. My curiosity was in overdrive, and I eventually put aside all thoughts of getting any work done at the office. I drove back to the den site only to receive yet another surprise. There in the field, approximately half the distance from where I had been, both foxes were slowly scanning the ground with their noses, searching for their lunch.

I pulled over and grabbed my binoculars to make a closer inspection. The animals combed the field for several minutes before the larger of the two suddenly sprang into the air and landed several feet away. I then watched the two foxes take turns tossing the captured rat into the air. After a few minutes, the smaller one ended the rat's torture for good. It consumed a portion of the rodent and then allowed its mate to finish the meal. They continued hunting the field for another hour before returning to the den.

Several weeks later, the year's first snowfall covered the landscape, and it seemed like a good time to check on my new friends again. It would prove to be quite an eye opener.

The sky was gray and promised more snow as I walked around the field inspecting fox tracks. It soon became apparent to me that the two predators weren't venturing beyond a mile of the den. This was odd behavior, because it's common for red fox to have home ranges exceeding several miles in diameter. In fact, it has been estimated that some foxes travel up to one hundred miles from the birth den.

I spent several hours following animal tracks that day. In addition to those of my foxes, I saw quite a few coyote and bobcat tracks, along with tracks from several other animals. I followed winding track lines through the fields to nearby backyards, a Dumpster, and a construction site. The animals were apparently hunting the fields while traveling to and from possible handout areas, where they were feeding on scraps left by humans. Torn hamburger and candy wrappers at the construction site were evidence of the foxes' feast. Pet food dishes in some of the backyards revealed their liking for Little Friskies cat food. But I didn't form my plan for luring the foxes in until I discovered three different piles of meadowlark feathers.

The following day, I finished lunch, gathered my snow camouflage, camera, and electronic game caller, and headed to the field. I positioned myself inside a brushy fenceline adjoining a field approximately eight hundred yards from the den site. Here, I began playing a meadowlark distress tape at medium volume.

The sounds of the distressed bird had been playing for fifteen minutes or so when I noticed the fox. The beautiful red fur first appeared like a drop of blood on the snow as the animal emerged from the den. Seconds later, the second one appeared. I adjusted the binoculars and began spying on the animals. They moved about very cautiously for several minutes before the larger of the two began trotting toward me. As if on command, its mate came behind it.

Soon the foxes were within a hundred yards of the snow-covered speaker box. I slowly began preparing the camera, being careful to contain my excitement. Then, without any apparent reason, both foxes stopped and stared in my direction.

The tension mounted while I watched the animals begin moving side to side. Moving very slowly, I reduced the sound level down to where I could barely hear it. This prompted both foxes to again cautiously stalk the speaker. I aimed the camera at the targets and cut off the caller. The foxes continued to advance on the silent speaker. They were now within thirty yards, and I had exactly the situation I wanted. The only thing that could possibly have gone wrong did—the camera failed me.

But I'd learned some valuable lessons from those little foxes, which led me to many successful encounters with others later on.

THE GRAY FOX

The gray fox (*Urocyon cinereoargenteus*) has a head and body that average twenty-one to twenty-nine inches. The tail is bushy

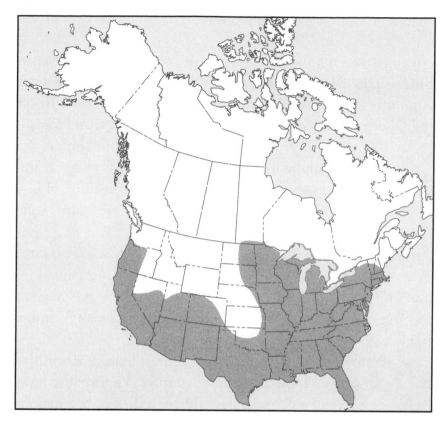

Gray Fox Range

Although smaller, the gray fox is much bolder than its red cousin. (FWS)

and runs eleven to sixteen inches. It weighs a slight seven to thirteen pounds. The coat appears as a mix of salt and pepper, with buffy underfur and a black stripe running down the length of the body. The sides, neck, back of the ears, legs, and feet are a rusty-yellowish color. The tail is usually tipped in black.

Gray fox generally mate from mid-February through March and deliver four to seven pups after an average gestation of fifty-one days. Grays will den in hollow logs, in ground burrows, beneath boulders, or in other forms of shelter.

These foxes eat small mammals and birds, but will also feed on insects, fruits, acorns, and bird eggs. They are capable of climbing trees to escape danger or destroy bird nests. Grays are also known to doze among the branches of trees while sunning themselves during periods of extreme cold.

Grays usually prefer more dense terrain than reds, but they may be found in almost any type of country. Their home range averages around one or two miles, although they've been known to travel over fifty miles from a documented release point.

Unlike the red fox, the gray isn't known for its shyness and will readily respond to predator calling. They are often the first animals to appear at the calling site. Hunters should know that this animal is usually easy to lure back with a different call if the primary target does appear to scare it off.

COURAGEOUS GRAY

The sounds of a jackrabbit in distress had cut through the darkness for only a minute or so when I detected movement. The dark shape appeared in pale moonlight, and I immediately knew it was a gray fox. Its fast-paced, nose-to-the-ground approach made identification easy, even at night.

The little predator quickly approached and moved beneath the pickup, coming out on the other side. This behavior persisted for several minutes while my companion continued calling. When the spotlight came on, the bold little creature simply sat on its haunches and stared at us. We ignored it and went on calling, hoping to coax in a better prize. After several minutes of listening and watching, the little fox got up and trotted off into the night.

Nothing else showed up after half an hour of calling, so I began a series of high-tone lip squeaks. Hopefully, the gray fox would return and I could try my luck with a .22-caliber pistol. The glowing eyes of the fox appeared just a few minutes later. After a momentary pause, it again came to within mere feet of the truck. My companion produced a soft whistle while I took the easy shot.

It's possible to view this story as another example of why the gray fox is thought to be the dumbest of predators. But I disagree. I think the gray fox has to be bolder simply to compete effectively with other predators. If it can get to an easy meal first, it can make

Grays have a reputation for responding quickly to calling, particularly at night. (FWS)

off with it before larger predators arrive. Thus, when calling specifically for gray fox I prefer the distress sounds of small prey. Bird and rodent distress sounds seem to be the top producers, but I've had numerous grays respond to distress calls from gray fox pups while calling for coyotes. So always be prepared for a response when calling in the land of the courageous gray.

THE RACCOON

Most hunters don't really consider the raccoon a predator. But they certainly are in this hunter's opinion, and should be hunted as such. Raccoons are notorious for destroying bird nests. They

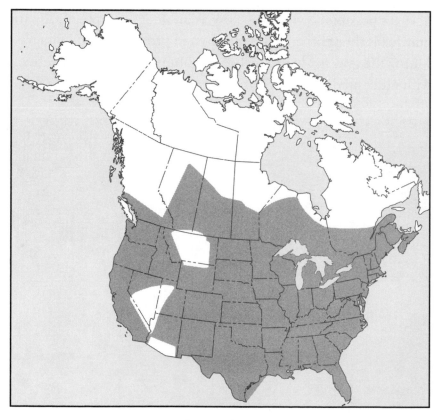

Raccoon Range

also raid the burrows of small game animals. On many occasions, I have discovered strong evidence of where a raccoon has raided and destroyed a nest of young rabbits. Add in the destruction to wild turkey, pheasant, and quail nests and you're darn right I hunt the masked bandit as a predator.

Raccoons vary in size depending on region. Body lengths range from eighteen to twenty-eight inches, while tails average just under a foot. Mature raccoons run twelve to thirty-five pounds. The body color is a mixture of pepper and salt, but the black mask on its face and the alternating rings of yellowish-white and black on the tail make it easy to identify. Raccoons have five toes on each foot, non-retractile claws, and walk on the entire foot.

The young of the year are born between April and May after a gestation period of approximately sixty-three days. Only one litter is born annually, with an average of four young. Dens may consist of hollow trees, logs, rock crevices, or ground burrows. Populations may run from one per acre to as high as fifteen per acre.

Raccoons are chiefly nocturnal creatures, but they're occasionally abroad during daylight. They feed mostly along streams, lakes,

Raccoons are often overlooked as predators, but they can do quite a bit of damage to other wildlife populations.

185

and other water sources, and will eat fruits, nuts, frogs, crayfish, bird eggs—virtually anything available. Raccoons are famous for dunking their food in water before eating it.

HUNTING THE BANDIT

The most common method of hunting raccoons is with the help of hounds. Many of my fondest memories are of nights spent following a pack of hounds in hopes of treeing a raccoon. Today, I prefer to call these creatures to the gun.

I really didn't look at calling as an effective approach until I began to notice the number of 'coons that responded to my fox calls. In fact, when hunting in prime raccoon habitat, I discovered they would respond even more readily than fox. So I did a quick check on the legality of raccoon calling and began taking advantage of the given opportunities.

While they are often hunted at night with dogs, raccoons will also respond readily to the sounds of distressed birds.

I soon found that the best sounds for luring raccoons were birds in distress, particularly distressed woodpecker and meadowlark. It pays to be ready for an encounter, though, because raccoons are among the boldest of animals, especially if provoked. So I began carrying a .22-caliber sidearm for such occasions.

Years went by and I continued to cash in on Mr. Bandit whenever and wherever I could. Then I discovered the Johnny Stewart Fighting Raccoons tape. I was hunting on the edge of a large swamp the first time I used the new sound. It was in the wee hours of the morning, and a light fog was coming from the swampy waters inland. A depleted battery and the fog restricted the range of my headlamp. Any encounter I had was going to be a close one, and I knew it.

Within moments of turning on the Fighting Raccoons, a pair of silver-colored eyes appeared like glowing diamonds in the dark. And they were moving toward me very quickly. I brought the advance to an abrupt halt with a blast from my shotgun.

The reflecting eyes continued to mark the animal's location while I scanned the light around my perimeter. Just then I felt something crash into my left foot. Naturally, this frightened the living daylights out of me, and I responded by leaping several feet into the air from a sitting position and shouting. When I returned to earth I placed my foot directly on top of a big raccoon. The animal didn't take kindly to this and let me know it by attacking my heavy rubber boot.

For several seconds, the scene was full of confusion, growling, and cussing before each party was able to pick a line of retreat. But during my escape I managed to rip the wires from my headlamp and crash into a tree. The collision and sudden darkness didn't help my state of mind any. Luckily, my backup flashlight had fresh batteries, and I was able to gather my stuff (and my wits) and navigate out of the swamp.

Hunters looking for excitement should definitely try calling these bandits of the woods. They generally provide fast action, within ten to fifteen minutes of starting the caller. I'd also advise you to always inspect nearby trees, as raccoons will sometimes climb up to inspect the scene. And don't forget to watch your back when dealing with a masked bandit—I certainly never will again.

Chapter

16

HUNTING THE BOBCAT

Dark clouds blanketed the sky, and snow drifted down on the wind. A tingle of excitement warmed my chilled body as I scanned the brushy surroundings. Only the squawking of a blue jay disturbed the silence, reinforcing my suspicion that something was coming in. The electronic game caller continued the agonizing cries of a distressed kitten. After a minute or so, I silenced the caller.

Tension mounted while I peered over the muzzle of the shotgun I had slowly positioned in the direction of the noisy blue jay. Carefully, I began scrutinizing every bush, leaf, limb, and weed for a clue to confirm my suspicions, which years of experience had led me to.

Several minutes passed before I could distinguish a pair of large yellow eyes peering from behind a bush. I adjusted the muzzle of the gun so that the fiber-optic TruGlo gun sight rested on the piercing yellow eyes. A tap of the finger released the safety and I squeezed the trigger. The powerful magnum shattered the silence, and only the bobcat's light-colored belly fur marked its presence inside the brush. Another bobcat, one of nature's most proficient and prolific predators, was in the bag.

CAT FACTS

The bobcat (*Felis rufus*) is found exclusively in North America and is the most common of all wildcats. The name is derived from their stubby (bobbed) tail, which rarely exceeds six inches in length. The tail appears tawny brown or grayish, with black bar markings and a black tip and pale white fur underneath. Male bobcats are usually about a third larger than females. Adults measure twenty-eight to fifty inches long and fourteen to seventeen inches high at the shoulder. Weight can range from fourteen to sixty-eight pounds, depending on sex and geographical location.

The track of the bobcat is easily distinguishable, as the front and hind prints are almost the same size—about two inches across, with four toes and no visible claw impressions. The bobcat's heel print is lobed at the rear and slightly concave in front, giving it scalloped front and rear edges.

The secretive bobcat is always a special prize. (Sue Weddle)

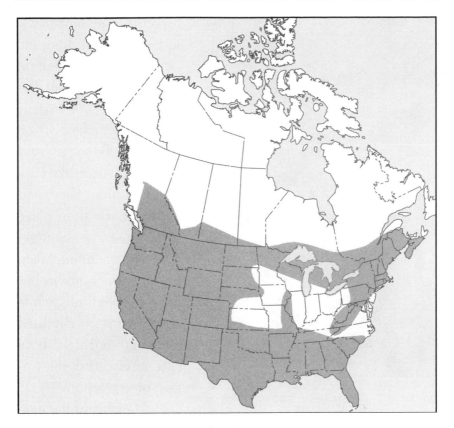

Bobcat Range

The bobcat's trail is usually very narrow, and its back feet often land on or overlap the tracks of the front feet. When trailing a bobcat in good media (e.g., snow, sand, or mud), always be on the lookout for their distinctive scent posts. The cats establish these signposts by scratching and urinating at a designated location for the purpose of marking their territories. Bobcats often use tree trunks for scratching posts. These markings can often be found near a cache of food the cat has buried and covered with sticks, twigs, leaves, and other ground cover.

Bobcats prey on a variety of small animals, including hares, rabbits, squirrels, porcupines, and rodents. Birds such as quail,

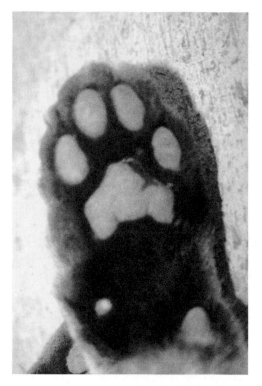

The bobcat's foot is much rounder than a coyote's, and the claws aren't usually visible in the track impression.

turkeys, pheasants, waterfowl, and domestic poultry also rank high on the menu. These smaller prey species are usually eaten immediately on capture. Bobcats may also attack deer-sized animals, which they partially eat and then place in a cache. These larger animals are often taken from ambush sites in low hanging tree limbs, while small prey is captured after a ground stalk. Bobcats rarely feed on carrion or vegetation.

They begin the mating process during late winter or early spring, depending on geographical location. Gestation averages approximately fifty-six days, with litters producing one to seven kittens. The young are usually born in protected areas such as rocky shelters, small caves, hollow logs, or abandoned buildings. Birthing areas are lined with dried leaves, grasses, and other dry vegetation. Kittens appear light brown in color and are spotted.

Bobcats are relatively predictable within their home range, as they often use the same pathways for routine travel. This is particularly true close to the den site or at water crossings. Bobcats are not overly fond of water, but if pressed, they will swim.

These cats are primarily nocturnal creatures and like to move on the edges of low-light periods. But like any wild animal, they are unpredictable and may be seen at any time. Bobcats are secretive in their movements and usually stick to some form of cover when traveling.

HOUNDING BOBCATS

The use of trained hounds is an effective means of hunting bobcats. Hounds detect the scent of the bobcat and pursue it, chasing the cat into a tree or an elevated position. Once the cat is treed, the hounds keep the bobcat at bay until the hunter arrives.

While hunting with hounds can be very exciting, I'm not all that crazy about chasing after a pack of dogs anymore. Father Time has slowed me down, and besides, I find it more thrilling to have the cat come to me than to chase it all over the countryside.

Predator hunters often bag bobcats and coyotes from the same stand location.

LURING TO THE GUN

Luring bobcats into gun range with a predator caller is probably the most common method of hunting. The hunter simply produces the sounds of a distressed prey animal and then waits for the bobcat to come in. Sounds simple, doesn't it? Well, it probably sounded simple to the thousands of hunters who tried it and then quit in frustration. In reality, luring a bobcat can be one of the most challenging feats in the hunting world.

Bobcats often seem to wear a dunce hat one minute, and then, in the blink of an eye, hang it on the hunter. I've watched some bobcats stand around while multiple gunshots were fired at them; shots that knocked debris in their faces before they died or finally retreated. And I've seen other cats bolt for no apparent reason.

While hunting at night on one occasion, I observed a large bobcat sitting and watching the beam of the spotlight. The cat sat perfectly still for several minutes, moving only its head as it followed the light like it was some kind of show. Naturally, the cat's amusement led to its demise when I finally decided I wasn't looking at a stump in the darkness. Instances such as this have reinforced my belief in the old saying "curiosity killed the cat."

Watching so many bobcats approach calling sites only strengthens my belief in the curiosity factor. I can't count the times I've seen a bobcat appear a hundred yards or so away and then sit down and stare in my direction. Nothing I do with the caller can coax the cat a single inch closer. After thirty to forty-five minutes, the cat simply rises and wanders off as if nothing ever happened.

On many occasions, however, the opposite has occurred. I've had a bobcat stare me in the face before I even completed the first calling sequence. In fact, there have been times when I wondered if I actually sat down beside the bobcat without know-

Some cats make themselves easy targets, while others are as careful as anything in the woods.

ing it. They are extremely unpredictable in responding to a call, which often spares them from the hunter's bullet, because so many hunters are predictable. Hunters usually remain at a calling site for a set number of minutes and leave as soon as the time is up. Often as not, the bobcat watches the hunter depart without the hunter ever knowing it.

CURIOUS KITTIES

There was a time when a man could trade a stack of prime pelts for a fistful of hundred-dollar bills. Like a lot of guys in those days, all my spare time was spent trying to collect fur.

Any wild critter packing a pelt was living dangerously back then, particularly the bobcat, whose coat could bring in hundreds of dollars. So when I'd rise from an unproductive stand only to see a bobcat scurrying into the brush, I'd be less than pleased. It was educational, though, and I quickly learned to be more patient.

Well-furred bobcats are still worth decent money.

Instead of spending the usual thirty minutes per stand, I increased it to forty-five minutes, which often netted a big tom late in the session. I also reduced the length of the calling sequence. I'd use a mouth-blown caller for approximately thirty seconds before allowing three minutes of silence. In most cases, I detected my target during the silent periods.

In a week's time I had collected three more bobcats, all during my final minutes in the stand. I was making more money and learning a valuable lesson about never underestimating these predators. This lesson was really driven home one cold morning when I spotted a nice red fox responding to my call.

The fox had appeared on a small mound of dirt approximately sixty yards in front of me. I quickly placed the scope's crosshairs on the critter, and with the crack of the .222 Remington cartridge, it tumbled over the mound. Only the white tip of the dead animal's tail remained visible.

I left it there and continued my calling routine. Then, with the designated time expiring, I became silent. Several minutes passed before I suddenly detected movement inside the brush before me. I knew instantly that it was a bobcat stalking in the usual manner. But this cat was stalking in the direction of the fox instead of toward me.

Amazed at its behavior, I continued to watch the cat. Not even the sounds of my lip squeaking disturbed the cat's advancement. After several more minutes of sneaking through the brush, the cat suddenly stopped. Then it dawned on me that the cat had actually been stalking the fox's tail. I also realized that the cat was now close enough to see what the white furry object was attached to.

Thinking back, I wish I had given the bobcat a little more time before dropping the hammer. But I'd already seen clear proof of its curiosity, which would help me bag these animals for years to come.

VISUAL AIDS

In my opinion, trappers, really good trappers, are the finest hunters. They must not only locate their game, but also lure the animal to a precise position. This usually requires some form of lure or decoy. In bobcat trapping, the use of a visual attractor can make all the difference. For example, a single bird feather hanging above the trap is an excellent aid for gaining success.

For hunters, visual attractors might come in a number of forms; anything from a single feather dangling in the air to a life-sized decoy. In fact, I have even used a small piece of tissue paper to lure predators from hiding. Anything that creates motion in the breeze will catch a bobcat's attention, just like the furry white tip of the fox's tail I mentioned earlier.

The key is to place the attractor so that it lures the animal into a shooting position, while diverting its attention away from the hunter. In most instances, I place the attractor approximately twenty-five yards in front of my calling position. But I have shot a few cats when situated closer to the decoy. They often stop short of the mark, and then sit down and stare at the decoy. So the hunter should always watch the areas surrounding the decoy, instead of looking directly at it.

FINE TUNING

The bobcat's sense of smell is probably the poorest of all the predators. But what it lacks in nose it more than makes up for with eyes and ears. These capabilities are among the keenest found anywhere in nature.

A bobcat's eyes can detect the slightest of movements. I firmly believe that some cats have spotted me from a single blink of my eyes. I once watched a bobcat traveling along a brushy fenceline that suddenly leaped sideways into the undergrowth.

Bobcats have keen eyesight and usually stalk their prey with caution. (Sue Weddle)

Seconds later it emerged with a bobwhite quail fluttering in its mouth.

This super-keen eyesight probably defeats more hunters than anything else. Hunters have a tendency to move while on stand, turning their heads or shifting their hands. Movement of any sort should always be restricted, especially while calling.

The distressed sounds of almost any creature will attract a bobcat. I've lured them in with distressed rabbits, rodents, and birds. But in recent years, the sounds of a domestic cat in trouble have really been a good producer. I think this is due to the increasing number of feral cats now competing with bobcats. I also think volume matters more than the type of sound.

Hunters have a tendency to hear only what they want to hear. They seem to forget that most predators have hearing capabilities far beyond their own. This usually results in the hunter calling with excessive volume, which in turn represents an unnatural situation to any animal within listening range. I think this is the primary reason why animals stop short of the calling location. Think about it. How many humans can hear the distress sounds of a rat sitting fifty yards away? Well, bobcats can, so when you blare calling sounds across the landscape, they know something isn't right.

To hunt bobcats successfully, the hunter must be as savvy as the intended target. These animals survive through their secretive nature, and the hunter should never forget it.

BECOMING A GOOD CAT HUNTER

Throughout this book, I share many tips and tactics for becoming a predator hunter, but when it comes to bobcats a few factors stand above everything else. First, you must become a student of cat behavior. Felines do things differently than canines. They are more cautious in their movements, and very patient. Good hunters learn to identify these actions and use them to their advantage. Observing a domestic cat stalking its prey is a great way to get a feel for how most bobcats behave on the hunt.

Patient hunters have the best success with bobcats.

I have spent hours at my office window watching a common house cat stalk a bird or squirrel. Their movements are always in sync with those of their intended prey. I have also noted that the closer a responding cat gets to a sound source, the more cautious it becomes. This applies to all predators in the cat family. Use this knowledge when you're working a calling location, and you'll bring home more bobcats.

Chapter
17

HUNTING LARGE PREDATORS

BEARS

The sun had retreated to the western horizon, and dark shadows engulfed the dense New Brunswick woods. It was now prime time for bushwhacking the big bruin my outfitter had told me about. This was my first hunt for black bear, and I was thoroughly caught up in the moment.

I moved only my eyes in scanning the area around the fifty-five-gallon drum of bait. The foul odor of the canister's contents informed me that the wind was in my favor. The tension mounted with every sound, real or imagined, and I had a sense that something in the dark woods was watching me.

But nothing happened before shooting time ran out; I could no longer see the crosshairs of the rifle in the dim light. I unloaded the rifle and began descending from the elevated platform. I was about halfway to the ground when all hell broke loose below me.

Startled, I flew back up the ladder. How I managed to crawl back onto the platform, reload the rifle, and avoid a heart attack I'll never know. Never before had I heard such horrifying sounds of pain and anguish.

As suddenly as it had begun it was over, and an eerie silence took its place. I couldn't decide which was worse. Something deadly was out there, and I had no intention of facing it in the dark.

Soon, I spotted the glow of the guide's flashlight knifing through the blackness. He had instructed me to stay at the site until he came to pick me up. Man, was I ever glad to see that gentleman and his light. I vowed never again to be caught out without my own flashlight, no matter what anyone advised.

As soon as my feet touched earth again, I began relating to the guide what had just occurred. I could hear him chuckling as we hastily retreated from the area. Once we had climbed into the warm pickup, he told me what had probably happened.

He said that it wasn't uncommon for a large male bear to kill a cub of its own species. This usually happens during the fall, after the female has abandoned the youngster before hibernation. Big boars are very territorial, and the cub had probably just followed its nose to the bait at the wrong time. It seemed as good a reason as any for the frightening episode.

A CALL IS BORN

That trip ended with me barely getting a glimpse of the big bear on the final afternoon of the hunt. But the sounds of that unlucky cub echoed in my memory—and still do. I used these memories to collaborate with my good friend and game-call maker David Hale. In a short time, we fashioned a caller that imitated the sounds of a distressed bear cub.

The following year I returned to New Brunswick, hoping to lure in a big bear with the experimental caller. I told my outfitter about my intentions and asked his opinion. Just as I expected, he was somewhat doubtful about its chance for success, but he reminded me that it was my hunt and I should give it a try if I wanted to.

After some thought, I elected to use the new caller only during the final minutes of the day. It would be a last-ditch effort in the event that the bait didn't bring a bear in during shooting hours. This was the compromise I had come up with after hearing the outfitter's polite reservations.

The five-day trip had run its course without much happening, and it was now the final day of hunting. I had ended every evening with at least five to ten minutes of distressed cub calling. As my guide had predicted, nothing responded to the pathetic sounds I created with the caller. Failure was already heavy on my mind as I entered the platform treestand for the last hunt.

I loaded the Remington Model 700, checked the focus of the scope, and retrieved the caller. There were only two hours of daylight left, so I figured I had nothing to lose in trying the caller. I finished a calling sequence and then let things quiet down for a few minutes. Only the squawking of a raven sounded through the woods as I prepared to start another thirty seconds of calling. Just as I placed the caller to my lips, I detected a sound.

I listened intently for some confirmation of what I'd heard. I was about to chalk it up to a vivid imagination when I heard it again—the deep, guttural grunt of a bear. I immediately produced a couple of low-volume whines with the caller, and was rewarded with the sound of something heavy crashing through the underbrush. Then I saw black fur as the bear emerged into the small clearing. I snapped the rifle into position and waited, tense with excitement.

Time seemed to stand still as I peered over the riflescope at the bear. Only the sound of my pulse pounding in my ears disturbed my thoughts as I tried to judge the bear based on everything I'd read and been told. Finally, I focused the bear in the scope and pulled the trigger.

It reacted to the report of the .35 Whelen's 200-grain bullet by momentarily dropping in its tracks. But before I could chamber another round the bruin had regained its footing and vanished into the brush. I could only stare at the spot where I had last seen it. Slowly, the reality of what had happened sank in, along with the thought of what might still happen before I recovered my trophy.

I stayed on the platform nearly half an hour before climbing down. Should I wait for my guide to return at nightfall or pursue the bear alone? After inspecting the bear's blood trail, I elected to go ahead alone.

Very slowly, I began following the crimson trail through the thick undergrowth. I examined every inch of the jungle-like terrain before taking each step. It was a tense situation, and raw fear filled my thoughts as I inched ahead. After what seemed like a lifetime, I spied the hind foot of the bruin in heavy weeds, then the entire body.

The author with one of the first bears he called in.

I fired an insurance shot that would also direct my guide to the location. I was now a full-fledged killer of bears. Unfortunately, all the photos of this trophy disappeared along with my camera on the return trip.

BEAR FACTS

Bears, whether black, brown, grizzly, or polar, are the largest North American predators. While it's possible to hunt the other bears in certain geographic locations, most hunters across the continent will be putting their crosshairs on the black bear. So this is the species we'll focus on.

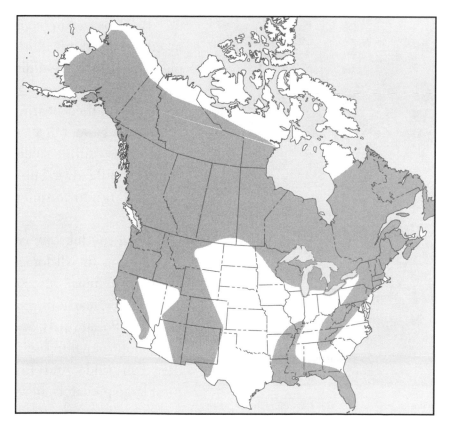

Black Bear Range

Black bears range from 200 to 475 pounds or more and often measure over six feet from nose to tail. Pelt color varies from charcoal black and cinnamon to almost blond.

They may den up beneath fallen trees, in hollow logs, caves, or anywhere shelter can be obtained. In colder regions, black bears semi-hibernate during the winter months. These animals are usually nocturnal, but can be found out and about at almost any time of day. Their range extends from the mountainous areas of the West, up through the far north, and across the heavy woodlands and swamps of the East and Southeast.

Color-phase bears, like this cinnamon taken by Murray Burnham, aren't uncommon. (Jim Zumbo)

Black bears can reach speeds exceeding thirty miles an hour for short distances. Their eyesight is only fair and their hearing moderately good, but their noses are quite keen. Hunter should always take these factors into consideration.

Food can take almost any form, as they'll forage for berries, nuts, insects, eggs, honey, carrion, garbage, small mammals, and just about anything else they can find. And like most large predators, black bears will occasionally take domestic livestock.

Where legal, black bears are usually hunted over bait or with hounds during spring and fall seasons. But in recent years, some states have banned these methods and/or the spring season for bear hunting. Hunters have had to revert to spot-and-stalk tactics or other methods. And some hunters are beginning to recognize the importance of using a predator caller for luring their trophies.

CALLING BEARS

My first experience with bear calling—not counting the minor experiment I tried on my earlier bear hunt—came by accident. I was again in New Brunswick, but this time I was hunting for whitetail deer. The bear season had closed just prior to my arrival, so I wasn't even thinking about them.

I managed to take a fairly nice buck on the second day of the hunt, which left me with four days to fill hunting waterfowl and coyotes. In the mornings, I concentrated on ducks and geese, and coyotes were my main target later in the day.

Waterways often provide hunters the opportunity to reach prime bear country without making noise. (J. Wayne Fears)

But I received one heck of a surprise at the beginning of my first coyote hunt.

I had taken a stand position on the edge of a large clear-cut near a beaver swamp. The sounds of my first calling sequence had barely subsided when I heard a crashing sound coming from the swamp. I thought that perhaps a pack of coyotes was charging toward me, so I directed the muzzle of my .223 Remington at the noise. Excitedly, I prepared for the coyotes to emerge from the thick undergrowth. But my excitement quickly vanished when a big—and I mean big—black bear busted from the cover.

Shock froze all the muscles in my body. My eyes must have been the size of dinner plates, and you probably could have shoved a football into my gaping mouth. To put it mildly, I was scared senseless.

For a moment, the bear just stood and stared in my direction. Then it began to look over its shoulder. Never in my life have I been so happy to see an animal turn and walk away.

COONEY ON BEARS

Judd Cooney is a noted outdoor writer, photographer, hunter, guide, and outfitter. He is, in my opinion, one of this era's top outdoorsmen. During a professional get-together of sorts, I told Judd and some friends about my New Brunswick calling experience. Keep in mind that this was back in the days before anyone, to my knowledge, had written anything about calling bears. Judd told me I was lucky the bear didn't have me for supper.

In his dead-serious manner, Judd told me about his experiences luring bears with a predator caller. The advice he gave me was based on first-hand experience, and anyone who wants to have success in this vein should take it seriously.

First, Cooney recommends using the coarsest tone possible for calling black bears. Modified jackrabbit-in-distress callers work well, as do specialty callers like the Burnham Brothers Magic and the Knight & Hale Ultimate 1. The latter callers produce a gravelly sound bears seem to prefer over standard rabbit-in-distress sounds.

Judd also advises hunters to call aggressively because bears seem to have very limited attention spans. So unlike some forms of predator calling, bear calling should be continuous until you're ready to shoot. Pausing during the calling sequence just allows them to become distracted.

Calling aggressively works well on bears. (Jim Zumbo)

COUGARS

Mountain lion, cougar, puma, panther—call it whatever you want, but *Felis concolor* is the largest of the wild cats found in North America. Primarily a creature of the night, it's hardly ever seen during daylight hours. The cougar is very secretive in its movements, often existing very close to humans without being detected.

A mature cougar averages around forty-two to fifty-six inches long, with the trademark tail running another three feet or so. Cougars weigh from eighty to two hundred pounds or more, de-

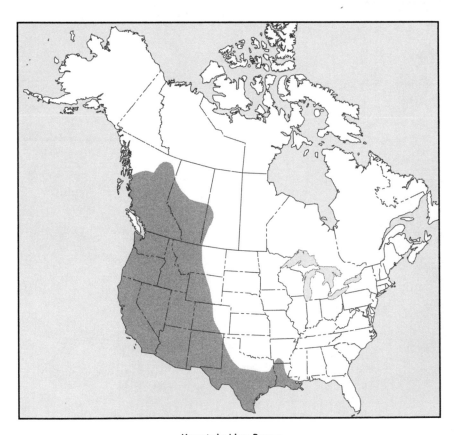

Mountain Lion Range

It's rare to catch a cougar off guard in broad daylight. (Sue Weddle)

Treeing cougars with the help of trained hounds is the most popular method of hunting, but the big cats can also be lured to a call.

pending on geographical location. They have a tawny to grayish appearance, with dark brown on the tip of the tail, back of the ears, and the sides of the nose.

Cougars primarily live in rugged mountain areas, forests, and swampland. They live mostly on the ground but will climb trees, especially to evade dogs. Cougars largely feed on deer, but will also take smaller animals such as rabbits and hares. They occasionally feed on domestic livestock, including cattle and horses, and often cache uneaten portions of their kills, although they won't eat tainted meat.

Dens are usually in concealed, sheltered locations. Cougars may give birth to young during any month of the year, after a gestation period of eighty-eight to ninety-seven days. They hear well and see even better, although like most cats, their olfactory senses are poor.

The most common method for hunting cougars is with the use of hounds. Cougars may lead a pack of hounds for several miles before taking refuge in a tree. Hunters should always prepare themselves physically before attempting this style of hunting, as it's exciting but exhausting.

CALLING COUGARS

Hunters often ask me if cougars will respond to a predator caller. My answer is always the same: Yes. Like any predator, they'll respond to the distress sounds of a possible meal. However, cougars are generally very slow and cautious in their approach. In most cases, I doubt the hunter ever even realizes a cat has come in to the call.

I have, on a few occasions, discovered cougar tracks near my calling site as I'm leaving the location. They appeared to be very fresh, and I felt sure they were made while I was calling. How something the size of a cougar could sneak in and out without ever being seen is beyond me, but I know they have.

On at least four occasions, I've actually spotted cougars responding to my calling. Unfortunately, on all but one hunt, the law protected the big cats and I had to pass on these golden opportunities.

BAD-TIME BOB

The night was especially dark, even for south Texas. Only the glow of the spotlight proved my eyes were open. Cries of agony emanated from my partner's Burnham Brothers Black Magic caller as he worked the light around our position.

Slowly, the blue lens revealed the desert surrounding us. Suddenly the beam of light stopped, and I heard my partner whisper, "Cat." I peered through the riflescope, trying to find the bobcat he'd spotted.

I could see nothing at first, but then with a single step the cat appeared in the crosshairs. I fired just as it stepped between prickly pear plants. The big bobcat leapt straight up into the air, spun around, and headed back in the direction from which it had come. Even before my friend spoke the words "gut shot" I knew what I had done, and a sickening feeling quickly came over me.

My companion rapidly swept the perimeter with the light, but we caught only a quick glimpse of the fleeing bobcat—and then something happened. From the darkness we heard the worst sounds imaginable. Screams of pain echoed across the desert.

My companion and I stopped in our tracks and then retreated back to the truck. The horrifying screams of the bobcat sent chills through us, and we were at a loss as to what to do next. Finally, all was silent, which somehow seemed deafening to our ears after the noises we'd just heard.

The now-uncovered searchlight sent its beam through the darkness, and the muzzle of my rifle trailed behind it. We were quiet for several minutes and then my partner asked if I'd ever heard anything like that before.

"Hell, no," I said.

We mulled things over for another fifteen minutes or so and then worked up the courage to investigate. Cautiously, we walked in the direction of the commotion we had heard. Soon our flashlights were playing over tattered pieces of bobcat fur lying on the ground. There wasn't much to do but return in the daytime to give the area a more thorough investigation.

The next morning we found ample evidence that my poorly shot bobcat had run into a cougar. Numerous fragments and dried blood spots revealed that the cougar had literally ripped the bobcat to sheds.

We thought long and hard about what we would have done in the face of a nighttime cougar charge. But in the end, the only thing we knew for sure was that cougars were fond of eating bobcats. This knowledge would later aid me in other encounters with the big cats.

CATS OF CONTROVERSY

There is a lot of controversy surrounding cougars these days. Some states have banned cougar hunting completely, but in many places cougar numbers are growing. Attacks on humans are becoming more frequent in these protected areas, and the animals exhibit little fear of Man.

Anti-hunting groups have managed to keep the cats off-limits in many areas, but the rising number of injuries and fatalities begs the question of how much is too much. When will they turn to hunters to rein in these populations?

I suspect that we'll soon be asking the same question about the reintroduced gray wolf.

Cougar populations have rebounded in some areas, but attacks on humans are also on the rise. The animal's secretive nature allows it to move unseen very close to human activity. (FWS)

THE GRAY WOLF

The reintroduction of the gray, or timber, wolf (*Canis lupus*) in several western states has really gotten some folks upset, and rightfully so. The federal government planted breeding pairs of gray wolves among some of the nation's best big game herds. These wolves quickly multiplied and expanded their range.

While they were released on public land in Yellowstone National Park and on national forest land, these areas are surrounded by private land owned by hard-working people who must protect their livestock. Unfortunately, these large predators don't distinguish between such lands, or between livestock and wild game. How is a growing wolf population going to affect these people?

The wolf is already proving it can influence big game populations. Many of these elk and deer herds were in trouble until

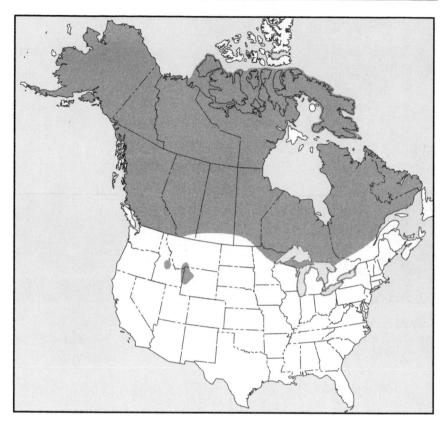

Gray Wolf Range

sportsmen began pouring countless dollars into restoring their numbers. Now the government is turning wolves loose on the fruits of this labor. This makes no sense to me. In fact, it seems like a slap in the face to a lot of dedicated hunters.

There is much debate about how these predators should be dealt with. At present, the federal government appears ready to turn over management to the states affected, but first they want to pass judgment on each state's plan for the wolves. In particular, Wyoming still has a different opinion about how best to manage these critters. If you ask me, a lot of sportsmen's dollars went down the drain in creating this dilemma, so sportsmen should get something in return—like a nice wolf to mount.

HUNTING THE BIG CANINES

I have collaborated with numerous Canadian wolf hunters over the years. Most of these outfitters hunt wolves over bait, with snowmobiles, or from some type of ambush. A few have told me that they sometimes get a wolf to respond to

Not everyone is happy about the gray wolf's return to the West. (FWS)

a predator caller if a bait site is within the immediate area. But as most wolves travel in packs, standard calling methods probably won't be too effective.

Ambushing is probably the best method for hunting these large canines. With the way things are shaping up in the lower forty-eight states, it might not be long before American predator hunters have a chance to find out what works and what doesn't.

Hunters in extreme southern regions of the United States could encounter another species of wolf: the red wolf (*Canis niger*). This subspecies is smaller than the gray wolf, averaging just under fifty inches long and carrying a thirteen- to eighteen-inch tail. The southern wolf may weigh anywhere from thirty to eighty pounds and appears reddish-gray to nearly black in color. This wolf is often mistaken for a coyote.

Professional hunter Jim Zumbo with a trophy timber wolf. (Jim Zumbo)

Predator hunters may encounter a red when calling. In my opinion, which is shared by other hunters, the red wolf will respond just as readily as the coyote. The trick is knowing which species you're looking at. The red wolf is protected by law, even in areas were it isn't supposed to exist.

DON'T SHOOT! I DON'T EXIST

A few years back I was hunting with a good friend on some public land. It was an extremely cold and cloudy morning. We had made one stand where I had let the air out of a single coyote and let another make a fool of me.

We then walked approximately a half-mile to a spot I had hunted several times over the years. Coyote tracks were usually plentiful along the old logging road, but not this time. In fact, there was hardly any coyote sign at all. I was puzzled by this, but still wanted to try my old hotspot.

The red wolf looks a lot like a coyote. (FWS)

I set up my FoxPro caller to play the sounds of a gray fox in distress, and before long I detected something dark coming through the woods. I readied my rifle, thinking I was about to bust another coyote. But something wasn't right; the animal in front of me was very large and almost black in color. Instantly, I knew I wasn't looking at a coyote unless it had been feeding on some kind of super-fortified diet.

The animal continued to narrow the gap, and was soon standing about twenty yards away. I could easily see the bright red collar around its neck, which supported a small black box. I peered over the riflescope, and fought the overwhelming urge to trip the trigger.

Slow seconds ticked away as we stared each other in the eye. Its eyes were different from any other animal I'd ever encountered. Suddenly, the large canine turned and began trotting way, and I noticed it didn't tuck its tail under as a retreating coyote normally does. The tail stayed level with the body.

I halted the caller and shouted for my partner to come over. My expression immediately told him something was off, and I quickly related the encounter. After casting around, we found the animal's tracks in some soft dirt. We inspected them carefully and agreed that they were the biggest coyote tracks we'd ever seen. We also agreed that the depth of the tracks indicated an animal larger than an average coyote.

We spent the rest of the day trying to locate the official that oversaw the property. We told him of our findings, and pointed out on a map where the incident had occurred. He proceeded to tell us how foolish we were, that no such creatures existed in the area, especially with radio collars.

We weren't inclined to thank him for his time, so instead I asked him what he would have done to me if I had shot the imaginary animal and brought it to him. This instantly wiped the smirk off his face. He narrowed his eyes, reddened a bit, and barked, "I would have arrested you."

So if you ever encounter something that "doesn't exist," think about the consequences before pulling the trigger — or keep your experiences to yourself.

Chapter
18

CARING FOR YOUR TROPHY

Humans have used animal skins for clothing and shelter since the first beast fell to a spear or club. Fur was a major impetus for exploration around the globe. It was a valuable commodity and played an important role in the founding of our country. Only in recent years has the price of fur really declined dramatically. But even with their loss of commercial value, skins are always of some worth to the hunter.

In addition to what income they still bring in, pelts make beautiful garments and decorations. So it's vital to care for the skin properly on harvesting the animal.

Unlike some hunters, I don't begin skinning right away. First, I remove any blood, dirt, burrs, or other debris found in the fur. I have also discovered that it helps to apply a good dose of insect killer to the corpse and seal it in a trash bag for a few hours. This reduces the number of fleas or other parasites commonly found on fur-bearing animals.

GEARING UP

Being prepared will save you a lot of time and trouble. My skinning kit is as valuable to me as my gun and caller. In most

223

Using the right tools will make the job of skinning much faster and smoother. (Monte Burch)

instances, I skin my animals in the field, which allows me to dispose of unwanted carcasses.

The first equipment necessary for skinning most small predators is a pair of rubber or latex gloves. Always wear gloves when you handle an animal, because certain diseases can be transmitted through small cuts on your hand, or even chapped skin. You can wash and reuse them, and sprinkling a bit of baby powder inside helps get them on and off.

Your skinning knife should be razor sharp, and be kept that way during skinning. I always have a sharpening stone handy when I'm skinning. Fixed-blade or folding knives work fine, although I prefer the folding type with multiple blades. These knives provide more options in blade length and style.

Suspending the animal from a small skinning gambrel makes the job much easier. If a gambrel isn't available, you can anchor the animal to a tree limb by running rope through the back legs.

I carry some plastic trash bags for storing the pelt after skinning. And for obvious reasons, I also bring a roll of paper towels and a bar of antiseptic hand soap.

TWO WAYS TO SKIN

There are two methods for skinning predators: open pelt and cased skinning. Which one is best in a specific situation will depend on the animal's size and how you plan to use the skin. Large predators such as bears, wolves, and cougars will be open skinned, as this is the preferred method for rug making.

Open skinning is also used for pelts that will be tanned immediately, without being dried or placed on a hide stretcher. This method requires more incisions to the animal, as the skin will be removed to expose the entire underside of the pelt. This is also the best skinning style for home decoration.

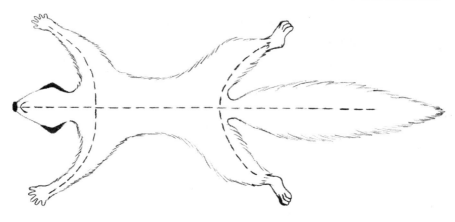

Recommended cuts for open skinning.

Open skinning is also the method most taxidermists favor for life-size mounting. But skinning for taxidermy purposes requires great precision. Eyelids, lips, ears, nose, and feet all must be carefully skinned to ensure a life-like appearance. Whenever possible, let the pro do the skinning on a trophy mount. If you have to do it yourself, be patient with the knife.

Cased skinning is the best method if the skin will be put on a hide stretcher and dried for storage. Hunters who collect fur to

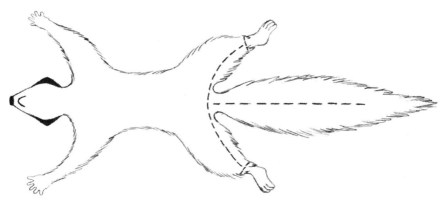

Recommended cuts for cased skinning.

sell at the end of the season like this approach. The hide is removed from the animal by peeling and cutting it away from the carcass, which leaves the pelt inside out on completion.

PREPARING THE PELT

Once the pelt is free of the carcass, inspect it again for blood and debris and clean if necessary. In most instances, I carefully brush the pelt with a pet-grooming tool to fully remove debris. Next, look for any damage from cuts and/or bullet holes, and repair these areas with needle and thread. When this is finished, remove all flesh, fat, and meat from the underside of the pelt, which is called "fleshing" the skin.

Use a fleshing beam and knife for this task, and drape the hide fur side down over the beam. With the dull side of the fleshing knife, use a firm push stroke to roll the material off the hide. Remove all unwanted material, paying special attention to the legs, neck, and head.

The next step isn't really crucial, but it often pays off—washing the pelt. The cleaner the pelt is before it dries, the better the finished product will appear. And this step usually increases the value of the pelt to the buyer. Washing involves nothing more than mixing a mild solution of dishwashing soap and warm water in a bucket. Prime pelts usually get a bath with a common hair

Fleshing is an important step in preserving the hide. (Monte Burch)

Softening the skin. (Monte Burch)

shampoo. Place the pelt in the bucket and gently wash the skin for several minutes. Then rinse it in another bucket filled with clean, cold water.

Next, remove the hide and twist it to remove excess water. Turning the skin inside out and shaking it vigorously will usually do the trick. If not, use an old bath towel to pat it dry.

STRETCHING

Pelts that will be sold are usually dried on a hide stretcher. These can be purchased in wood or metal and are sized for various species of game. It's important to use a stretcher that matches the animal.

Metal stretchers are made of springy wire that can be compressed to help in sliding the pelt over the frame. Be sure the pelt is centered on the stretcher and that the head fits snugly on the top of the stretcher. Now attach one of the stretcher's metal hooks through the skin at the base of the tail, about half or three-quarters of an inch from the edge. The teeth of the other hooks are then fastened to the skin of the back feet. Pull the arms down to tighten and stretch the skin.

When the pelt dries the hooks are removed and the metal stretcher is again compressed to release the pelt. Most predator pelts are dried with the fur to the inside. However, the pelt can be reversed after it has partially dried.

Wooden stretchers are more traditional. Do-it-yourselfers can fashion them from pine shelving boards. Wooden stretchers provide an advantage in that they allow the tail to be spread out and pinned in place. The basic procedure is the same as with metal stretchers, but once the pelt is in place standard pushpins are used to attach it to the stretcher.

These skins are dry and have just been removed from stretchers. (Monte Burch)

DRYING

Pelts must be dried properly to achieve the desired results. Hang them upright in a protected area with temperatures between forty and sixty degrees. Drying will take three to seven days, depending on temperature and humidity. Once the pelts are completely dry, they can be removed from the stretcher and stored in a cool, dry place. I would also advise keeping the pelts suspended to avoid possible damage from mice and rats. Furs being sold to buyers are dried without the use of salt or other preservatives.

DO-IT-YOURSELF DECORATIONS

Tanning your pelts to make rugs or garments can be fun and rewarding. As I mentioned earlier, I prefer to use open skinning for pelts that will be tanned. I would also recommend saving and cleaning the animal's skull if a rug mount is desired.

There are a lot of ways to tan a hide. Tanning solutions range from a mixture of salt and alum to a host of commercial varieties. I've used Deer Hunter's Hide Tanning Formula from Cabela's and Tannit from the Tandy Company. These products come with instructions and a complete tanning kit. I'd recommend them to anyone who prefers simplicity to serious work.

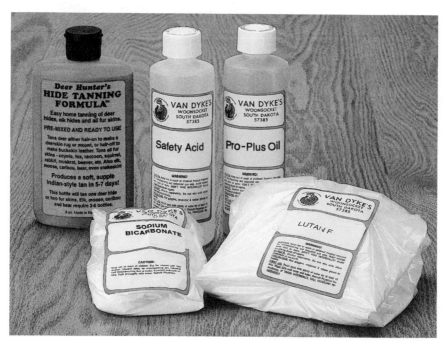

Commercial products make tanning much easier. (Cabela's)

If you're planning a full skull rug, you'll need some Dakota Modeling Clay to shape the skull for a natural appearance. If the actual skull couldn't be saved, it's possible to buy a commercial substitute. When it's in place, insert a pair of glass eyes in the sockets and your rug mount is ready. All of the products and accessories you may need can be obtained from Van Dyke's Taxidermy Supply Company (1–800–787–3355 or van dykestaxidermy.com). If you are new to skinning and tanning, I'd also highly recommend obtaining a copy of *The Ultimate Guide to Skinning and Tanning*, by Monte Burch, published by The Lyons Press. This book has information on leather making, as well.

Here a skin is being soaked in a pickling solution. (Monte Burch)

TAXIDERMY TIPS

Many hunters like to admire their trophies in the most life-like state possible, which means it's taxidermy time. And how the trophy is cared for will influence the finished product. I have seen

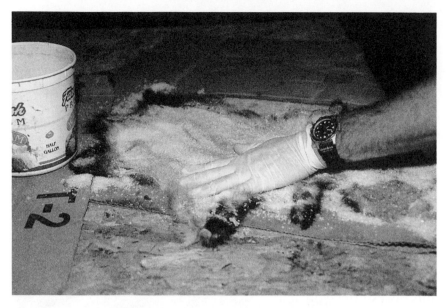

Tanning takes some patience but is worth the effort. (Monte Burch)

many a splendid mount spoiled simply because the hunter failed to do a few simple things.

Start by cleaning the fur carefully in the field. This procedure may have to be repeated several times before the animal is actually delivered to the taxidermist, but it's worth it. If you head afield with a trophy in mind, don't forget a roll of paper towels. These can be used to wipe away fluids and should be placed inside the animal's mouth, nostrils, and wound area to absorb excess blood.

Animals should be kept as cool as possible and out of direct sunlight. This helps prevent fur slippage due to putrefaction, which begins with the animal's death. If you can't get to the taxidermist within twenty-four hours, think about freezing the skin. Simply wrap the animal in a few layers of plastic trash bags and place it in a deep freezer. But even with freezing, you should make every effort to get to the taxidermist quickly to avoid possible freezer burn.

FINAL THOUGHTS

Today, predator hunting is one of the fastest growing shooting sports. But the place of the predator hunter in modern society is changing, so it's particularly important to be aware that how we present ourselves may be instrumental to the very future of our sport.

Proper care during skinning will leave you with a beautiful trophy. (Monte Burch)

True hunters accept defeat as a learning experience and view success as a reward for patience and skill. If we lose our love for the hunt, and respect for our prey, we have lost the advantage in being the ultimate predator.

INDEX

A

Age, 30
Ambush sites, 130, 135
Ammunition
  used as reward, 16
Animal Damage Control
  coyotes, 3
Arizona, 120

B

Bait, 154
  bears, 205
  hunting over
    illustration, 134
Baiting, 133–135
  landowners permission, 133
  location, 133
Ballistics, 41
  balancing, 42–44
Bansner, Mark, 38
Battery terminals, 29
Bears, 203–211. *See also* Black bears
  attacks on humans, 4
  bait, 205
  calling, 210–211
  photograph, 206
.218 Bee, 42
Behavior
  bobcats *(Felis rufus)*, 200–201
Binoculars, 48
  photograph, 49
Bipods, 50
  photograph, 50

Bird distress calls, 184
Birds, 70
Birth
  bobcats *(Felis rufus)*, 192
  cougars *(Felis concolor)*, 214
Black bears
  calling, 209–210
  coat, 208
  dens, 208
  feed, 208
  photograph, 208
  range, 208
    illustration, 207
  size, 208
  speed, 208
Bobcats *(Felis rufus)*, 149, 189–201
  behavior, 200–201
  birthing, 192
  calling, 196, 197
  distressed sounds, 198
  eyes, 197
    photograph, 198
  feed, 191–192
  foot
    photograph, 192
  gestation, 192
  hounds, 193
  luring to gun, 194–196, 197
  mating, 192
  photograph, 190, 193, 195, 196
  preying example, 7
  range, 190
    illustration, 191

Bobcats *(Felis rufus) (continued)*
  scat
    illustration, 68
  sense of smell, 197
  signposts, 191
  size, 190
  tracks, 190
    illustration, 67
  trail, 191
  visual aids, 197
Bolt action rifles, 38–40
  photograph, 39
Bounty Hunter calling machine, 22, 85–86
Breeding
  coyotes *(Canis latrans)*, 96
.243 bullet, 40
Bullets, 44–45. *See also* specific bullets
  weight and design, 41
Burch, Monte, 231
Burnham, Murray
  photograph, 76
Burnham Brothers, 22, 86
Burnham Brothers Black Magic caller,
  215
Burnham Brothers Magic, 211
Burnham Brothers predator caller, 18, 20
Bushnell, 51
Bushnell rangefinder, 162
Bushrag Ghillie Suit
  photograph, 54

C
.22 caliber bullet, 40
.22 caliber centerfire, 40, 42
Calling, 75–92
  bears, 210–211
  black bears, 209–210
  bobcats *(Felis rufus)*, 196, 197
  cougars *(Felis concolor)*, 214
  with enthusiasm, 77
  game, 18–19
  location, 89–92
    photograph, 90
  natural manner, 77
  pitfalls, 76–80, 79, 211
  presentation, 77
  raccoons, 187
  sequence, 80–81
  techniques, 87–88
  volume, 83, 153
Calling machine
  Bounty Hunter, 22, 85–86
  electronic game, 85–87
Calls
  selecting, 81–84

Camaraderie
  rewards of predator hunting
    photograph, 12
Camouflage, 54–56
  photograph, 88
Canadian wolves
  Yellowstone National Park and Idaho
    photograph, 11
Canis latrans, 3
Carrion, 133
Cartridge
  photograph, 41
Cased skinning, 225, 226
  illustration, 226
Cat
  tracks, 65
Chickens, 16
Choke
  shotguns, 51
Closed reed calls, 82
Close range coaxer, 21, 148
Clothes
  hunting, 54–56
Coat
  black bears, 208
  gray fox *(Urocyon cinereoargenteus)*, 182
  raccoons, 185
Cold, 154
Colored lens, 157
Concealment
  calling, 89
Contender, 53
Cooney, Judd, 210
Cougars *(Felis concolor)*, 212–213
  attacks on humans, 4
  birth, 214
  calling, 214
  dens, 214
  habitat, 214
  hounds, 214
  photograph, 213
  range
    illustration, 212
Cover
  photograph, 91, 144
Coyotes *(Canis latrans)*, 93–103, 105–112
  breeding, 96
  characterization, 6
  dens, 96
  feed, 96
  gestation period, 96
  location, 95
  Los Angeles, California, 2–3
  mating, 96
  migration, 97–98

new horizons, 96–99
pelts, 94, 110
photograph, 3, 22, 95, 97, 100, 124
physical characteristics
    photograph, 132
range
    illustration, 94
removal of, 7–8
scat
    illustration, 62
    photograph, 61
snatching pets, 4
social behavior, 103
tracks
    illustration, 63
traps, 110
urine, 111
Crap, 61

D
Dakota Modeling Clay, 231
Dark, 156–157
Decoys
    fawn deer, 161
Deer decoys, 161
Deer Hunter's Hide Tanning Forumla,
    230
Dens
    black bears, 208
    cougars *(Felis concolor)*, 214
    coyotes *(Canis latrans)*, 96
    gray fox *(Urocyon cinereoargenteus)*, 182
    raccoons, 185
Diet
    scat, 61
Digestive waste, 61
Dirt hole set, 110
Distress callers
    jackrabbit in, 210–211
Distress calls
    bird, 184
    rodent, 184
Distressed sounds, 137
Dogs. *See also* Hounds
    hunting coyotes, 137–138
    photograph, 138
Domestic livestock
    photograph, 6
Dougherty, Jim, 22
Dung, 61

E
Eastern hunters
    photograph, 115
Eastern predators, 123–130

Ecotone, 128
    photograph, 129
Electronic game calling machines, 85–87
    photograph, 86
Encore, 53
E.R. Shaw, 38
Eyes
    bobcats *(Felis rufus)*, 197
        photograph, 198
E-Z Howler caller, 136, 139, 150

F
Fawn deer decoys, 161
Feed
    black bears, 208
    bobcats *(Felis rufus)*, 191–192
    coyotes *(Canis latrans)*, 96
    gray fox *(Urocyon cinereoargenteus)*, 182
    raccoons, 185
    red fox *(Vulpes fulva)*, 175
Finger wigglers
    calling, 80
Firearm safety, 34
Fixed power, 47
Flat shooting cartridges, 41
Fleshing
    photograph, 227
Focused, 32
Foot
    bobcats *(Felis rufus)*
        photograph, 192
Footwear, 56
Foxes
    robbing nests, 7
    snatching pets, 4
FoxPro, 131, 136, 221
    photograph, 86
Fur
    cleaning, 232

G
Game calling, 18–19
Gear, 35–56
Gestation
    bobcats *(Felis rufus)*, 192
    coyotes *(Canis latrans)*, 96
    raccoons, 185
Glacier National Park, 10
Glove box, 29
Gray fox *(Urocyon cinereoargenteus)*, 180–184
    coat, 182
    dens, 182
    feed, 182
    habitat, 182
    mating, 182

Gray fox *(Urocyon cinereoargenteus) (continued)*
    photograph, 181, 183
    predator calling, 182
    range
        illustration, 181
    scat
        illustration, 67
    size, 182
    tracks
        illustration, 66
    Gray wolf *(Canis lupus)*, 217–222
    hunting, 219–220
    photograph, 9, 219
    range
        illustration, 218
    restoration, 11
Guides, 118–120
    advice, 119–120
    photograph, 119
    reputation, 119

H
H. S. Precision, 38
Habitat
    cougars *(Felis concolor)*, 214
    coyotes *(Canis latrans)*, 95
    gray fox *(Urocyon cinereoargenteus)*,
        182
    red fox *(Vulpes fulva)*, 175
        photograph, 176
Hale, David, 204
Handguns, 53
    photograph, 53
Harris Bipod, 162
Health
    scat, 61
Hen turkeys, 161
Hicks, Gene, 15
Hornady, 44
.17 Hornady Magnum Rimfire, 46
.22 Hornet, 42
Hounds
    bobcats *(Felis rufus)*, 193
    cougars *(Felis concolor)*, 214
    raccoons, 186–188
Howling device
    photograph, 139
Human activity, 72–73
Hunters
    photograph, 125, 200
    thinking like predators, 128–130
Hunting clothes, 54–56
Hunting partners, 26–28
Hunting predators
    why, 1–13
Hunting rigs, 29–30

I
Intelligence
    genetics, 124
Itinerary, 30

J
Jackrabbit in distress callers, 210–211
Johnny Stewart Fighting Raccoons tape,
        187

K
Keith, Elmer, 16
Kentucky, 138–139
Kentucky Lake, 139
Knight, Harold
    photograph, 108
Knight & Hale calls
    photograph, 83
Knight & Hale Ultimate 1, 140, 151, 211

L
Barkley, 139
Land Between the Lakes (LBL), 138–139,
        167
Landowners
    photograph, 59
Large predators
    hunting, 203–222
Leopold, Aldo, 9
Litters
    raccoons, 185
    red fox *(Vulpes fulva)*, 175
Livestock attacks, 5
.22 Long Rifle rimfire, 46
Lost livestock disposition, 72
Lynx
    tracks, 65

M
Magic Park, 10
Manual caller, 159
    photograph, 78, 81
Map, 30
Marksmanship, 15
Mating
    bobcats *(Felis rufus)*, 192
    coyotes *(Canis latrans)*, 96
    gray fox *(Urocyon cinereoargenteus)*, 182
Mechanical calling, 85–87
Mental edge, 32–34
Mental practice sessions, 34
Mental preparation, 32
Metal stretchers, 228
Migration
    coyotes *(Canis latrans)*, 97–98
Mississippi River, 96

Missouri, 121
  coyotes, 105
Montana
  bounty on wolves, 9
Moose populations, 11
Mosley, Johnny, 38
Mountain lions
  See also Cougars
  preying on deer
    photograph, 4

N
Negligence, 25
Nighttime equipment, 157–158
Nighttime hunting, 156–157
  photograph, 158
Nosler, 44

O
Off season, 160–162, 163–164
  photograph, 161
Old Satan, 141–146
Ol' Dude, 137–138
Open garbage sites
  photograph, 73
Open pelt skinning, 225, 226
  illustration, 226
Open reed calls, 82
Opossums
  robbing nests, 7
Optics, 47–48

P
Page, Warren, 16
Partners
  hunting, 26–28
Pelts
  coyotes (*Canis latrans*), 94, 110
  drying, 229–230
  preparing, 227–228
  red fox (*Vulpes fulva*)
    photograph, 110
  stretching, 228–229
Physical conditioning, 30–32
Pickling solution
  photograph, 231
Politics, 9–12
Polycarbonate tipped bullets, 44
Poop, 61
Practice, 33, 44
Predation
  examples, 2
Predation victims
  photograph, 5–6
Predator cartridges, 40–41

Predator hunter, 38, 126
  benefits, 12–13
  competition, 126
  frame of mind, 128
  for hire, 7–8
  quality, ix
  unrealistic expectations, 127
Predator hunting competitions
  public land
    photograph, 169
Predator kill
  first experience, 17
Predator rifles, 35–38
  photograph, 36
Predators
  problems with, 5–6
  snow, 150
Preparation, 26
Prey animal tracks
  photograph, 71
P.S. Olt crow caller, 18–19
P.S. Olt predator caller, 20
Public land, 165–171
  hunting dates, 168
  photograph, 166
  planning, 166–168
  time, 168
Pursuing predators
  dividend, 7–8

Q
Quail hunting, 19

R
Raccoons, 184–188
  calling, 187
  coat, 185
  dens, 185
  feed, 185
  gestation, 185
  hounds, 186–188
  litters, 185
  photograph, 185, 186
  range
    illustration, 184
  robbing nests, 7
  size, 185
Rain, 147
Range
  black bears, 208
    illustration, 207
  bobcats (*Felis rufus*), 190
    illustration, 191
  cougars (*Felis concolor*)
    illustration, 212

Range *(continued)*
  coyotes *(Canis latrans)*
    illustration, 94
  gray fox *(Urocyon cinereoargenteus)*
    illustration, 181
  gray wolf *(Canis lupus)*
    illustration, 218
  raccoons
    illustration, 184
  red fox *(Vulpes fulva)*, 174
    illustration, 174
Rangefinders, 51
Reading signs, 60
Red fox *(Vulpes fulva)*, 173–175
  color, 174
  feed, 175
  habitat, 175
    photograph, 176
  killing rabbits, 7
  litters, 175
  pelts
    photograph, 110
  photograph, 17, 175, 177
  range, 174
    illustration, 174
  rebounding, 177–180
  scat
    illustration, 65
  tracks
    illustration, 64
Red wolf *(Canis niger)*, 219
  photograph, 221
  Relaxed, 32
.22/250 Remington, 42, 43, 165
  photograph, 42
.223 Remington, 42, 43, 210
  photograph, 42
.222 Remington Magnum, 42
Remington Model 700, 205
.280 Remington rifle, 146
.17 Remington rimfire, 46
Rhode Island Reds, 16
Rifles
  bolt action, 38–40
    photograph, 39
  predator, 35–38
    photograph, 36
  varmint, 37
    photograph, 37
Rodent distress calls, 184
Role reversal, 124–126

S
Safety, 15
  firearm, 34

Scat, 61
  bobcats *(Felis rufus)*
    illustration, 68
  coyotes *(Canis latrans)*
    illustration, 62
    photograph, 61
  gray fox *(Urocyon cinereoargenteus)*
    illustration, 67
  red fox *(Vulpes fulva)*
    illustration, 65
Scent, 56
Scent free soap, 56
Scopes, 157
  photograph, 47
Scouting, 57–73
  developing skills, 60–62
  photograph, 58
Sendero, 115
Sense of smell
  bobcats *(Felis rufus)*, 197
.17 Hornady Magnum Rimfire, 46
.17 Remington rimfire, 46
Shooting aids, 50–51
Shooting sticks, 50
Short magnum cartridge
  photograph, 43
Shotguns, 51–53
  photograph, 52
Signposts
  bobcats *(Felis rufus)*, 191
Size
  black bears, 208
  bobcats *(Felis rufus)*, 190
  gray fox *(Urocyon cinereoargenteus)*,
    182
  raccoons, 185
Skinning
  photograph, 224, 233
Skinning kit, 223–225
Skinning knife, 225
Skins
  photograph, 229
  softening
    illustration, 228
Snow, 148, 149–150
  photograph, 148, 149
Social behavior
  coyotes *(Canis latrans)*, 103
Southern coyotes *(Canis latrans frustor)*,
  95
Speed
  black bears, 208
Spotlights, 157, 194
  photograph, 159
Squeakers, 82

State regulations
  nighttime hunting, 159
Stewart, Johnny, 22, 86
Stuckey, Clay, 26–27
  photograph, 28
Swap the stop, 132–133
Swarovski, 51
.220 Swift, 42

T
Tanning
  commercial products
    photograph, 230
  decorations, 230–231
    photograph, 232
Tape recording
  screaming baby, 170
Taxidermy tips, 231–233
Temperature, 154
Tennessee, 138–139
Texas
  coyotes, 113–116
.35 Whelen, 206
3-D suit
  photograph, 55
Timber wolf
  photograph, 220
Tires
  air pressure, 29
Toolbox, 29
Topographic maps
  photograph, 167
Tracking media, 60
  snow, 150
Tracks, 62–67, 68–70
  bobcats *(Felis rufus)*, 190
    illustration, 67
  coyotes *(Canis latrans)*
    illustration, 63
  gray fox *(Urocyon cinereoargenteus)*
    illustration, 66
  prey animal
    photograph, 71
  red fox *(Vulpes fulva)*
    illustration, 64
Trail
  bobcats *(Felis rufus)*, 191
Trajectory, 40–41
Traps
  coyotes *(Canis latrans)*, 110
Treks
  photograph, 31
Trophies
  caring for, 223–233
TruGlo gun sight, 189

Turkeys
  hen, 161
.25/06 bullet, 40
.22 caliber bullet, 40
.22 caliber centerfire, 40, 42
.22 Hornet, 42
.22 Long Rifle rimfire, 46
.22/250 Remington, 42, 43, 165
  photograph, 42
.22 Winchester Rimfire Magnum, 46
.218 Bee, 42
.243 bullet, 40
.221 Fireball, 42
.222 Remington, 42
.223 Remington, 42, 43, 210
  photograph, 42
.222 Remington Magnum, 42
.220 Swift, 42

U
Ultimate Guide to Skinning, 231
Ultimate predator philosophy, 25–34
Urine
  coyotes *(Canis latrans)*, 111

V
Van Dyke's Taxidermy Supply Company, 231
Variable power, 47
Varmint rack, 115
Varmint rifles, 37
  photograph, 37
Velocity, 40, 41
Vest, 56
Visibility
  calling, 89
Visual aids
  bobcats *(Felis rufus)*, 197
Vultures, 70

W
Waterways
  photograph, 209
Weather, 147–154
  photograph, 148
Western coyotes *(Canis latrans frustor)*, 95,
    113–121, 114
Western hunting lands
  photograph, 120
Wild fur
  prices, 110
.270 Winchester, 40
.22 Winchester Rimfire Magnum, 46
Wind, 150–151, 152–154
  calling, 89
  photograph, 152, 153

Wolf Recovery in Yellowstone National Park
    and Idaho, 10
Wolves, 9
  Canadian
    Yellowstone National Park and Idaho
      p, 11
  eradication program, 9, 65
  preying
    photograph, 10

restoration programs, 9
tracks
  photograph, 69
Wooden stretchers, 229
Wootters, John, 16

Z
Zumbo, Jim
  photograph, 220